God Delivers On His Promise

13 Life-Changing Personal or Group Bible Studies

God Delivers On His Promise

13 Life-Changing Personal or Group Bible Studies

Editor

MELVIN E. BANKS, LITT.D.

Based on selected Old Testament Scriptures

Urban Ministries, Inc.

First printing 1989; second printing 1993; third printing 1994; fourth printing 1999.

Our thanks to Bennie Goodwin, Ph.D., Kenneth Hammond, Ed.D., and others who contributed to the writing of these life-transforming Bible studies.

Published in the United States by Urban Ministries, Inc.
P. O. Box 436987
Chicago, IL 60643
www.urbanministries.com 1-800-860-8642

ISBN 978-0-940955-56-1 (paperback)
ISBN 978-1-68353-667-3 (eBook)

Unless otherwise noted, scripture texts are taken from the King James Version of the Bible.

Cover design by Laura Duffy Design
Book design by Amit Dey

Printed in the United States of America.

This book is dedicated to Olive Banks, my devoted wife of many years. She has been a great encouragement to me as through the years we have worked together in the development of UMI. This book is also dedicated to Regis Scott Banks, my eldest grandson whose intelligence and sense of humor are my inspiration.

Table of Contents

Preface

How To Use This Book

The materials in these studies provide for in-depth exploration of the Scriptures. At the same time, we recognize that merely studying Bible texts as an end in itself is not adequate to accomplish all that should be accomplished.

The Scriptures make clear that God's purpose for people is that first they would come to know Him as Saviour (2 Peter 3:9), then go on to develop their relationship with Him so their lifestyles increasingly reflect the character of Jesus Christ (1 Peter 2:2).

We read in Romans 8:29 that God "predestinated [us] to be conformed to the image of His Son...." In other words, God's desire for believers is that they become more and more like Jesus Christ in character. We know that Jesus Christ is perfect and that we will never reach ultimate perfection in this lifetime. At the same time, we are encouraged to pursue the likeness of Christ. Note the purpose of each of the following sections which appear throughout the studies:

- DEFINING THE ISSUE
- AIM
- SCRIPTURE TEXT
- BIBLE BACKGROUND

- POINTS TO PONDER
- LESSON AT-A-GLANCE
- EXPLORING THE MEANING
- DISCERNING MY DUTY
- DECIDING MY RESPONSE
- LIGHT ON THE HEAVY

DEFINING THE ISSUE

These studies are designed to help people grow in their relationship with Jesus Christ, to foster discipleship. Each study begins with a section we call "DEFINING THE ISSUE." The purpose of this is to elevate a life need which will be addressed in the exploration of the Scripture text.

Scholars have observed that every book in the Bible was written to address a life need which the people experienced. Some books documented their history. Some dealt with false doctrine. Then, some books encouraged holiness of life.

AIM

This is a statement of what the study is designed to accomplish in the life of the participant. Aims can be modified to address the specific needs which the leader of the group senses to be those of the participant. A leader should never feel that the suggested aim has to be slavishly adhered to. The study is a "guide," not an unchangeable formula.

Some aims are structured to address the cognitive, emotional, and volitional components of behavioral change. Participants are encouraged to KNOW the truth, to FEEL deeply about the truth, and to take ACTION which reinforces the truth. All of which leads to a change in behavior and spiritual growth.

SCRIPTURE TEXT

This section includes a printed portion of Scripture upon which the study focuses. While the studies were prepared using the King James Version of the Bible, any version which the group prefers can be used. This section begins with an outline of the text which facilitates dividing the Scripture into smaller segments.

BIBLE BACKGROUND

The "BIBLE BACKGROUND" provides contextual material which can aid in understanding the people to whom the Scripture was originally addressed. It also explains the context for the Scripture portion, so that the text is easier to grasp.

POINTS TO PONDER

These questions are designed to help focus the minds of the participants on some of the areas that the study will address and to facilitate the understanding of the text.

LESSON AT-A-GLANCE

This section is an outline of the text which facilitates dividing the Scripture into smaller segments.

EXPLORING THE MEANING

Comments on the Scripture texts are found in this section. If possible, participants will have read the material prior to the gathering, so that reading entire sections is not necessary. However, the leader may want portions to be read in order to reinforce a particular point of discussion.

DISCERNING MY DUTY

Since the discussion of meaning should not be an end in itself, we have provided a section entitled, "DISCERNING MY DUTY." While in many cases, this allows the participant to think about the individual response to the Scripture, occasionally, this exercise may focus on group action. This is especially helpful if you think of your group as more than a "study" group. That is, your people will occasionally want to collectively engage in some activity which reinforces the aim of the study, and at the same time, promote the welfare of others.

DECIDING MY RESPONSE

Since there is a difference between knowing what could be done and actually doing it, "DECIDING MY RESPONSE" allows a participant to pinpoint what their response will be as a result of discovering what could be done.

We believe this approach to the study of Scripture will not only be exciting to all the participants but will result in real spiritual growth and discipleship.

LIGHT ON THE HEAVY

This section will provide additional information on a word or theme deemed helpful to the readers.

OTHER SUGGESTIONS

1. As a way of strengthening the bonds among the people within your group, you may want to plan some kind of social, once per quarter. This may consist of a potluck supper, a dinner/outing, etc.

2. You may also want to consider some form of ministry activity during the course of a study, such as:
   - Conduct a jail or prison service.
   - Make or purchase gifts for a public or private school class.
   - Do a special church cleaning.
   - Conduct a fundraising project for a missionary.
   - Gather clothing for needy children.
   - Write letters to a politician on a local or national issue of morality or justice.
   - Raise funds to send a needy child to a summer camp or on vacation.
   - Purchase books for your church library.

   A little time spent in your group brainstorming will produce lots of other ideas for serving the Lord and the people in a practical way.
3. You may want to use a portion of your time to allow your group members to pray for one another and for needs of the church.

Foreword

CELEBRATE 50 YEARS WITH US!

When UMI began in 1970, African Americans were still struggling to undo the effects of 350 years of slavery and Jim Crow segregation.

We believed both then and now that the more we know and rely on God's revelation in the Bible, the more we will be equipped to serve Him and to deal with racism, injustice, and to represent Jesus Christ in our world.

Three books, *The Unfolding Story of God's Salvation Plan*, *God Delivers on His Promise*, and *Good News about Jesus Christ*, are examples of UMI Bible studies that enrich our knowledge of God's Word. In these and other Bible studies, we explore not only our need for personal holiness but also God's standards for social justice and righteous living.

Since 1970, life has improved for many African Americans. Yes, we have a long way to go, but we see progress. Many churches have enriched their Christian educational programs. Surveys show that today a high number of young adults cling to the church and the Christian faith to help them cope with injustice and to live right. UMI's approach in presenting biblical truth improves total growth by offering Bible studies contextualized and professionally produced for African American children, youth, and adults.

It gives me great joy to see how God is using these materials to transform people for His eternal purposes.

It is clear that the mode of teaching is changing from analog to digital. This rapid change challenges churches to upgrade communication methods to accommodate digitized content. We know God's truth will never change because God is eternal truth. Still, our ways of teaching must adjust to a changing culture. For the 50th anniversary edition, these three books, which were originally published in print only, are now available as eBooks. We hope to see millions of more people come to love and live for our Lord in the years ahead.

African Americans are conscious of our African roots, and we seek to connect with brothers and sisters on the continent and in the African diaspora. Together, we can have a greater impact on the world for Christ and His eternal kingdom.

Carl Jeffrey Wright
Chief Executive Officer Urban Ministries, Inc.
Chicago, Illinois
September 8, 2020

Introduction

GOD DELIVERS ON HIS PROMISE

One of the exciting attributes of God is that He is the God of truth. All truth has its origin in Him and must be measured by Him. All truth exists for His eternal glory. The result of this great attribute is that God does not change.

What He says and promises is flawless. Since He has perfect knowledge of all that has been and all that shall be, He can make promises without fear of contradiction or failure.

This great attribute is demonstrated in His dealings with Israel. We have the privilege of looking back at how He dealt with these people, see how He made promises and kept them. Yes, He is God who keeps His promises. Observing how He kept His promises with them helps our faith today.

In Bible Study 1, we observe how God appeared to Moses at the "burning bush." God revealed His intent to deliver Israel from Egyptian bondage and promised Moses that proof of His intent was that one day Moses and Israel would be worshiping in that very spot "upon this mountain" (Exodus 3:12). Did God deliver on His promise? You bet He did.

In Bible Study 2, we observe the people crossing the Red Sea (Sea of Reeds) and Pharaoh, along with his army destroyed. "Israel saw the great work which the Lord did upon the Egyptians" (Exodus 14:31).

In Bible Study 3, we note how God made provision for this great company of people. Some estimate the number between 2-3 million. In the morning, God sent manna. In the evening, God sent quail which flew in and covered the camp. God provided food for the whole nation.

Bible Study 4 explores how God made a covenant with Israel. They would be His special people, a kingdom of priests, a holy nation. Despite repeated violations of the covenant agreement, God still owns His people. Does not God's faithfulness to Israel tell us that He will keep His promises to us?

In Bible Study 5, we observe how God gave assurance to the new nation. He promised He would be present with them. He instructed Moses to build a worship center, a tabernacle, where God would meet with Moses and with appointed High priests.

In Bible Study 6, we observe how God had a special concern for the poor within the nation. He decreed that every fiftieth year should be a time of jubilee, a time when what had been lost, people or land, would be restored.

In Bible Study 7, we observe how God established conditions for continued blessings from Him. After setting up the tabernacle, the place where the nation could commune with God, Moses conveyed to the people the kind of behavior that would ensure their continual bountiful crops, peace, and protection.

In Bible Study 8, we learn that Moses sent an expedition into the Promised Land. The report of 10 spies was discouraging. The report from Caleb and Joshua, however, encouraged faith to trust God for conquering the land. Important principles for seeking, finding, and doing God's will emerge from the study.

In Bible Study 9, a new generation of people are challenged to love God with all their hearts, souls, and might. They are reminded to remember God when they arrive in the land, lest after receiving great bounties, they forget God and turn to idolatry.

In Bible Study 10, we see Moses ending his illustrious career, unable to enter the Promised Land, after leading the people out of bondage and through the wilderness for 40 years. But he did not die (at God's instruction) before he appointed a new leader, Joshua. This assured the fulfillment of God's promise to give Israel the land.

In Bible Study 11, we explore how God kept His promise to be with Joshua as He had been with Moses. Joshua leads the people across the Jordan River where waters parted, allowing the multitudes of people to pass over on dry ground.

In Bible Study 12, we see how (at God's direction) the walls of Jericho fell, allowing the people to capture the city without "firing a shot." God again demonstrates His faithfulness and power of enabling these people to conquer the land.

In Bible Study 13, we see Joshua about to end his career, having led the nation in conquering the Promised Land, though much territory was still in the hands of the Canaanites. Joshua challenges the people to make a firm decision to serve the Lord.

Moses: His Call and Protest

Based on Exodus 2:23-4:17

DEFINING THE ISSUE

Among biblical heroes, Moses stands out as one of the greatest. Not only was he the instrument through which God provided a set of laws which are still the basis for the laws of most governments, but his personal life and experiences are both exciting to read and a challenge to follow. This study describes the manner in which God stepped into Moses' life to change and control it—to make it both satisfying to him and a benefit for generations to follow. Moses' experience is one which all of us should seek.

AIM

That participants may understand God is willing to guide them into ministries or vocations that are both satisfying to themselves and liberating to others.

SCRIPTURE TEXT

> EXODUS 3:1 Now Moses kept the flock of Jethro his father-in- law, the priest of Midian: and he led the flock to the backside of the desert, and came to the mountain of God, even to Horeb.

2 And the angel of the Lord appeared unto him in a flame of fire out of the midst of a bush: and he looked, and, behold, the bush burned with fire, and the bush was not consumed.

3 And Moses said, I will now turn aside, and see this great sight, why the bush is not burnt.

4 And when the Lord saw that he turned aside to see, God called unto him out of the midst of the bush, and said, Moses, Moses. And he said, Here am I.

5 And he said, Draw not nigh hither: put off thy shoes from off thy feet, for the place whereon thou standest is holy ground.

6 Moreover he said, I am the God of thy father, the God of Abraham, the God of Isaac, and the God of Jacob. And Moses hid his face; for he was afraid to look upon God.

7 And the Lord said, I have surely seen the affliction of my people which are in Egypt, and have heard their cry by reason of their taskmasters; for I know their sorrows;

8 And I am come down to deliver them out of the hand of the Egyptians, and to bring them up out of that land unto a good land and a large, unto a land flowing with milk and honey; unto the place of the Canaanites, and the Hittites, and the Amorites, and the Perizzites, and the Hivites, and the Jebusites.

9 Now therefore, behold, the cry of the children of Israel is come unto me: and I have also seen the oppression wherewith the Egyptians oppress them.

10 Come now therefore, and I will send thee unto Pharaoh, that thou mayest bring forth my people the children of Israel out of Egypt.

11 And Moses said unto God, Who am I, that I should go unto Pharaoh, and that I should bring forth the children of Israel out of Egypt?

12 And he said, Certainly I will be with thee; and this shall be a token unto thee, that I have sent thee: When thou hast brought forth the people out of Egypt, ye shall serve God upon this mountain.

BIBLE BACKGROUND

How God raises up a deliverer for His people is a fascinating series of events. Moses had to run away from Egypt (Exodus 2:15) so that his life would be spared from the Pharaoh's anger over his killing an Egyptian (Exodus 2:12). He found a place to live in Midian. While there, Moses married one of Jethro's seven daughters. During this time, Moses' people back in Egypt were under heavy bondage. God heard their cry for help. He was preparing Moses for the task.

This study deals with God's call to Moses to lead the children of Israel out of Egypt. The drama that unfolds in Exodus 3:1-12 gives insight into how God works in the lives of people like you and me. The end result never ceases to be a miracle.

POINTS TO PONDER

1. *What can you tell about Moses' life on the basis of your knowledge of shepherds?*

 ____

 ____

 ____

2. *What characteristics or attributes of God are indicated in Exodus 3:1-14? Name at least five.*

____

____

____

3. *What does "a land flowing with milk and honey" (Exodus 3:8) mean? Were the rivers filled with literal milk and honey?*

____

____

____

4. *What kinds of changes could Moses expect in his life when he changed occupations? What were the problems and pleasures of his life as a shepherd? As a leader of Israel?*

____

____

____

5. *What assurances did God offer Moses, if Moses took the job offered him?*

____

____

____

LESSON AT-A-GLANCE

1. *A bush that burned (Exodus 3:1-3)*
2. *A God who called (vv. 4-6)*
3. *A God who cared (vv. 7-9)*
4. *A task that awaits (vv. 10-14)*

EXPLORING THE MEANING

1. A bush that burned (Exodus 3:1-3)

Few people who read the Bible can forget the story of the burning bush. Children and adults alike are impressed with the miracle of a bush that burned but was not destroyed. Theologians see in this a symbol of the people of Israel, a nation placed in the fire of persecution but never destroyed. However we view the bush, there is no question that it was of great importance to Moses.

Exodus 2:1-25 summarizes the first 80 years of Moses' life. It describes some of his successes and failures. We find him at one point (2:10) being brought into the royal family of Egypt. We see him again (2:15) dejected and defeated. We read (2:21, 22) how he was able to "pick up the pieces" and go on to start a family and a new career. We find him patiently and persistently pursuing that career when God intervened to show Moses that he had not fulfilled his potential. There was still the good, acceptable, and perfect will of God for his life.

Moses was "content" (2:21) to live with Jethro, his father-in-law, and to pursue the occupation of a shepherd. It may have been that was all he wanted for his life. Security, some wealth, and a relatively easy life were sure to be his as a shepherd. However, there is little likelihood that he would have had a chance to help his own people or millions of others in subsequent generations had he remained in that comfortable position.

On the other hand, perhaps life as a shepherd was not completely satisfying to Moses. Maybe, as he went out day after day to care for the sheep, he had an inner discontent and a longing to be in some other place and position. It may have been that he longed to take up the task he had started earlier (2:11, 12), and be about delivering his brethren. But he may not have been sure where or how to begin.

Whether or not he was a bit discontented with his situation, Moses' life was about to be radically changed. The beginning of that change was marked by his seeing the bush burning but not being consumed.

Many adults today find themselves in positions similar to that of Moses, the shepherd. All too many teens are heading for such a fate. They are destined to spend a comfortable, but useless, life like his—or perhaps a life of misery, hoping and praying for a way out. Neither fate is the will of God for His children. An encounter with God can bring about change. God has many "burning bushes" through which He attempts to gain our attention. Some are written in His Word (cf. Revelation 3:20); others are part of our daily experiences. A pause, or a turning aside, could mean the difference between a fruitless, frustrating life, or a life of satisfying usefulness.

2. A God who called (vv. 4-6)

As Moses turned away from his preoccupation with the flock, God spoke to him.

A good teacher knows that getting attention is a prerequisite for any genuine communication. Advertisers recognize this principle and use it in radio, television, and in magazines. God uniquely attracted Moses' attention and then began to speak with him.

This was doubtless the first time Moses had heard God's voice. Of course, it was not the last time. From this point on, Moses was aware of how God can and does reveal His plans to people. God does communicate with those who tune in to Him. This is the first great truth of the "burning bush." Let us take heed to it.

Many believe that God is withdrawn and uninterested in the world which He created. Many argue that there is no divine revelation. They are convinced that God is silent or dead. Such may have been Moses' feeling before God spoke to him. This is the feeling of some young people who are trying to grab a handle on life today. Heaven seems to be brass. Let us be sure that if we turn aside and seek God, we will find Him already seeking us. We will find Him willing to speak—through His Word, through others, through experiences—as He did to Moses.

Moses also learned that God knew him personally. God called out to him, "Moses, Moses!" Nothing is more reassuring than being called by name. Nothing is more damaging to a personality than being unknown. Maybe you know how it feels to be in a strange place and suddenly have someone say your name. How delightful it is to know that you are known. How much better to know that God knows you! Jesus assures us that, "I am the good shepherd, and know my sheep" (John 10:14). Indeed, He reminds us that He "calls His own sheep by name" (John 10:3).

In spite of the glory and majesty of God, we can know Him and be known by Him. God calls and communicates His plan to people. Sometimes He has specific plans for specific people. That was true for Moses. His plan and purpose for Moses is recorded in Exodus 3:7-10. God brings together the task to be accomplished and the right person to do it. And if you keep focused upon His leading, God will bring you also to that particular task which is best suited for you.

The "burning bush" was the place where Moses learned that God knew and cared about him personally. Moses further learned that God must be honored by men. In his excitement, Moses rushed up to take a closer look at the burning bush. But he was stopped short by the voice of God telling him the conditions under which he might enter into God's presence. He was reminded that God is merciful and righteous, loving and just, kind and firm. God wanted to fellowship with Moses, but there were conditions which Moses had to meet. For instance, Moses had to respect the holiness of God.

Teens and adults alike today must understand that knowing God's will requires something from us. We must communicate with God. Taking off his shoes was a simple act for Moses, but it expressed a willingness to be obedient. Unfortunately, some people who express an interest in knowing the will of God are not obeying Him. They have not recognized God as sovereign. God made it clear to Moses at the outset that this new relationship was not merely a social interaction. God has to be Lord. God has to be honored and respected if the relationship is to proceed. This is still true for today.

3. A God who cared (vv. 7-9)

Moses had been forced to flee from Egypt because in his concern for the plight of his brethren there, he had committed murder. In his first encounter with God on the backside of the mountain, he discovered that the very thing which had troubled him was also of deep concern to God. Perhaps Moses had felt that God did not know or did not care about the conditions in Egypt. People were being forced to live in slavery. Children were being slaughtered. A nation was crying out to God for deliverance. Perhaps Moses felt that God was not concerned about these social and economic problems.

Whatever the doubts in Moses' mind, they were dispelled by God's own words. "I have surely seen the affliction of my people which are in Egypt, and have heard their cry by reason of their taskmasters; for I know their sorrows" (3:7). "I have seen . . . [I] have heard . . . I know their sorrows," God said. God revealed Himself as the God Who cares. Moses needed to be assured of this and share God's burden about people.

The parallel between the plight of Israel and that of other peoples and nations is very obvious. Spirituals sung by Black people before the American Civil War were often based on the experiences of Israel in Egypt. Whenever people have been enslaved, they have longed for freedom and have based their hopes on God's concern as expressed in Exodus, chapter 3. God declares His disapproval of oppression in no uncertain terms. He indicates His intention to deliver His people from such conditions.

We need only take a superficial glance at social and economic conditions around us to see oppressive conditions. Men use other people for the sake of economic gain. Men deny other men and women rights and freedoms which they want and demand for themselves. Men institute the caste system and classify individuals on the basis of ethnic or racial origin, using these classifications to deprive these people of rights and privileges. God expresses His displeasure at such behavior, whether in Egypt in 1700 B.C. or in 1999 A.D. In a world where injustice seems to be the rule rather than the exception, we should be encouraged to know that the God of all the earth is just and loves righteousness. God declared His intention to deliver the Israelites and destroy the Egyptians. Eventually the "wrong shall fail" and the "right shall prevail." We long for that time in our generation.

4. A task that awaits (vv. 10-14)

It is not difficult to imagine the excitement with which Moses listened to God's plan to deliver Israel. This was exactly what he had wanted. He was all for God's plan, until God said, "I will send you" (v. 10). Moses was to be the instrument through which God's will was to be carried out.

For Moses, this changed the picture. He would have liked God to deliver Israel by some miracle. But when he, Moses, had to do the job, it was not so easy to approve the plan. Moses must have vividly recalled the failure of his first effort to help his people. He knew full-well that he was now a fugitive because of that failure. He may also have thought of the problems of explaining God's plan to his wife and his in-laws, leaving his family, and giving up the security of his position.

Certainly, he had no army or other resources with which to carry out this bold plan. It was not false modesty when he said, "Who am I that I should go unto Pharaoh?" (v. 11) It is a fact that he was not, within his own means, equipped to bring Israel out of Egypt. Any military man could have told him so with only a superficial investigation.

Such feelings may grip us when we think of the work we must do. There are times when we have rivers that seem uncrossable and mountains we can't tunnel through. But, we must remember that God never assigns a task without giving the wisdom and strength to do it. "As thy days, so shall thy strength be" (Deuteronomy 33:25).

Still, Moses should have been encouraged by the commission. God invited him to "Come," and go to Pharaoh. He further assured Moses that He would go with him. What greater help is there than this? This means both psychological and material help. It is assuring to have a friend standing by when you face problems, even if the friend can be of no assistance. It is even more assuring to know that there is "a very present help in trouble" (Psalm 46:1).

God further assured Moses by promising that on the very mountain where they first met, the nation of Israel would worship God. It may have seemed incredible to Moses at that time, but this promise did indeed come to pass (Exodus, chapter 19).

Moses was also given credentials to present to his people. He was instructed to tell them that Yahweh, The Eternal God ("I AM") had sent him. Thus, God revealed for Himself a new Name—a covenant Name—which was from that time on to symbolize His nearness to His people. One could hardly hope for greater preparation than this. Yet, such resources are available to each of us, if we heed the call of God.

DISCERNING MY DUTY

1. *Moses' mission was to liberate his people Israel from Egyptian bondage. Is liberation still on God's agenda today?*
2. *Contrast and compare liberation as Moses would have understood it from the way Christians should understand that concept today.*
3. *In what ways can believers today be involved in a ministry of liberating people from social, physical, and spiritual bondage?*

DECIDING MY RESPONSE

Identify a person or family in your church or community in need of liberation from poverty, alcohol, loneliness, etc. Discuss how you as a group can be God's agent for liberating the person or persons. Take specific steps and report the results to your group.

LIGHT ON THE HEAVY

Horeb (3:1) is called the mountain of God by anticipation. In the Old Testament, Horeb and Sinai are used as equivalent terms. Although the former name may refer to the range of mountains, Sinai refers to a particular peak. It is impossible to know, with certainty, which of the many peaks, is the place where Moses met God, the highest rising to some 8,000 feet. (*Wycliff Bible Commentary*, p. 54)

God Brings Victory

Based on Exodus 13:17–14:31

DEFINING THE ISSUE

MRS. JONES: "Fred, you'll graduate from Park High this year, won't you?"

FRED: "No, ma'am. I'm going to drop out."

MRS. JONES: "Drop out? Why?"

FRED: "The school is dirty. The teachers are boring and the students are dangerous."

MRS. JONES: "Dangerous?"

FRED: "Yes, ma'am. Just last week, my friend, Leonard, got killed for his shoes and jacket."

MRS. JONES: "I'm very sorry to hear that."

FRED: "I am too, and I don't intend to lose my life for no shoes and jacket."

MRS. JONES: "I know, Fred. But isn't there any way you can stay in school one more year? You'll be finished next June."

If you were Fred, what would you do? Is there any way Fred can get victory over his fears? Is there anything Mrs. Jones, Fred's

Sunday School teacher, or the members of Fred's church can do to help make his school safer?

AIM

By the end of the lesson, participants will be able to clearly tell the story of Israel's journey through the Red Sea, will be able to express the significance of this partnership miracle, and will participate in the DECIDING MY RESPONSE (public school liberation) project.

SCRIPTURE TEXT

> EXODUS 14:21 And Moses stretched out his hand over the sea; and the Lord caused the sea to go back by a strong east wind all that night, and made the sea dry land, and the waters were divided.
>
> 22 And the children of Israel went into the midst of the sea upon the dry ground: and the waters were a wall unto them on their right hand, and on their left.
>
> 23 And the Egyptians pursued, and went in after them to the midst of the sea, even all Pharaoh's horses, his chariots, and his horsemen.
>
> 24 And it came to pass, that in the morning watch, the Lord looked unto the host of the Egyptians through the pillar of fire and of the cloud, and troubled the host of the Egyptians,
>
> 25 And took off their chariot wheels, that they drave them heavily: so that the Egyptians said, Let us flee from the face of Israel; for the Lord fighteth for them against the Egyptians.

26 And the Lord said unto Moses, Stretch out thine hand over the sea, that the waters may come again upon the Egyptians, upon their chariots, and upon their horsemen.

27 And Moses stretched forth his hand over the sea, and the sea returned to his strength when the morning appeared; and the Egyptians fled against it; and the Lord overthrew the Egyptians in the midst of the sea.

28 And the waters returned, and covered the chariots, and the horsemen, and all the host of Pharaoh that came into the sea after them; there remained not so much as one of them.

29 But the children of Israel walked upon dry land in the midst of the sea; and the waters were a wall unto them on their right hand, and on their left.

30 Thus the Lord saved Israel that day out of the hand of the Egyptians; and Israel saw the Egyptians dead upon the sea shore.

31 And Israel saw that great work which the Lord did upon the Egyptians: and the people feared the Lord, and believed the Lord, and his servant Moses.

BIBLE BACKGROUND

Moses eventually returned to Egypt as God directed him and demanded that Pharaoh let the Israelites go free. The Pharaoh hardened his heart and refused to let the people go. Whereupon God unleashed 10 plagues on the land of Egypt, some scholars think, to embarrass the Egyptian gods.

After the 10th plague, Pharaoh finally allowed the Israelites to go free and they set out on their journey. In the meantime, Pharaoh changed his mind; he decided to recapture his former slaves and came after them with his army, including a regiment of 600 special chariots (14:5-7). As the strike force got closer, the Israelites heard them and became so frightened, they cursed Moses for bringing them to the Red Sea to die (14:8-12). Moses told them to "fear not," but to "stand still and see the salvation of the Lord." He told them to take a good look at the Egyptians because this was the last time they would see them (14:13). The Lord gave Moses His instructions and our lesson tells what happened (14:15-20).

POINTS TO PONDER

1. *Moses' job to ________________ over the ____________. (Exodus 14:21, 26-27)*
2. *The east wind blew the seabed ________ so that Israelites walked between ______________ of water on __________ ground. (14:22)*
3. *The Lord parted the ____________, (14:21) troubled the ______ army (14:24), overthrew them in the midst of the __________ (14:27), and ________ Israel out of the hands of the ______. (14:30)*
4. *The Israelites responded to this miracle by ______ and _____ the Lord and ________ his servant Moses (14:31).*

LESSON AT-A-GLANCE

1. *The Lord guides Israel's escape (Exodus 14:21-22)*
2. *The Lord directs Egypt's defeat (14:23-30)*
3. *The Lord inspires Israel's faith (14:31)*

EXPLORING THE MEANING

1. The Lord guides Israel's escape (Exodus 14:21-22)

One of the truly great partnerships of Scripture is the Lord and Moses. Of course, the partners were not equal, but the partnership was effective because Moses did his little part and God did the rest. In our text, we see this process in action: Moses stretched out his hand over the sea and "the Lord drove the sea back with a strong east wind" (14:21, NIV).

In this episode, we see four things happening. First, we see Moses stretching out the rod (LB) in his hand out over the sea. When God gets ready to do something for us, there seems always to be a part for us to play. Whatever we can do, the Lord usually requests that we do it. God made the animals, but it was Adam's job to name them (Genesis 2:19-20). Jesus fed the 5,000, but not without a little boy's two fish lunch (John 6:1-13).

There are many medical, economic, and social problems in our churches and communities that are solvable, but we cannot expect God to do what we cannot do, unless we are willing to do what we can do. If we expect God to work the miracle that it will take to solve the problems, we must be willing to extend the hands that contain our resources.

Second, we see that God "opened up a path through the sea" (v. 21b, LB). Some writers have tried to explain away this miracle by saying that the "Sea of Reeds" was a shallow body of water or that the water stopped because of an earthquake. But, just like God expects us to do our part, we can expect God to do His part. And just as God used the East wind to dry up the sea bed, He could have used nature to cause the sea to open up. If He did, that does not detract from the miraculous uniqueness of the event. What made it a miracle was that it happened at the exact time it was needed. God was in direct control of what happened, when it happened, and why it happened. God has great variety. He uses whatever means His creativity deems necessary. When all the theories are imagined, we agree with Moses, who was an eyewitness to the event, "GOD DID IT!"

Third, the results of Moses' obedience and God's miracle was that the people were delivered. They "walked through the sea on dry ground" (v. 22, LB). How exciting! God seems sometimes to be single-minded in His determination to deliver His people. In spite of their fears and murmurings (14:10-12), and our faithlessness and disobedience, the Lord insists on loving us, forgiving us, and delivering us. He only requires that once the way has been made plain, that we walk into our deliverance.

2. The Lord directs Egypt's defeat (14:23-30)

A. What happened? The Egyptians were determined to recapture the Israelites and carry them back into slavery. Both their physical and mental vision were clouded. They were not able to see what was happening until it was too late.

It seems like they should have sensed that something extraordinary was happening when they saw the "walls of water." But they blindly pursued the Hebrews right into the Red Sea. It was only when God began to trouble or confuse (v. 24, NIV) them, making the wheels come off their chariots, that their eyes were opened. A perceptive Egyptian soldier yelled, "The Lord is fighting for the Israelites against us. Let us get out of here!" (14:25, TEV)

Unfortunately, it was too late. Moses held out his hand again and God let the walls of water drop back down into the riverbed and all of the Egyptian soldiers were drowned.

B. What shall we say about this? Well, first we say that it did not pay to fight God's children. God is always on the side of the oppressed. The oppressed are not always right. They are not always the most likable, the most spiritual, the most intelligent, or the most dependable, but they are the people with whom God identifies. They are God's people and we are warned not to offend them (Matthew 18:1-6) or neglect them (Matthew 25:31-46). In fact, Jesus dedicated His life to helping just such people (Luke 4:18-19). To fight these people is to put ourselves against God; to minister to them is to go into partnership with God.

   Second, as Christians, we must not celebrate the defeat of our enemies. It was appropriate for Moses and Miriam (Exodus 15:1-21) to sing about how God has defeated their enemies and made them sink "to the bottom (of the sea) like a stone" (15:5, TEV). But Jesus encourages us New Testament believers to love our enemies and to pray for our persecutors (Matthew 5:43). While we understand the jubilance of Moses, Miriam, and the others, who were delivered from slavery by the defeat and death of the Egyptians, we must reserve our celebration to the time when our enemies receive our Saviour and become new creatures in Christ (2 Corinthians 5:17). Then we can join heaven and rejoice over the sinners who have repented and the lost persons who have returned home (Luke 15:7, 10, 32).

3. The Lord inspires Israel's faith (14:31)

Aha! Here's something to rejoice about. Today's English Version (TEV) paraphrases verse 31 as "When the Israelites saw the great power with which the Lord had defeated the Egyptians, they stood in awe of the Lord, and they had faith in the Lord; and in his servant Moses."

A. "When they saw." What did they see? They saw a mighty miracle. Except for the miracle of salvation, the parting of the Red Sea is perhaps the most notorious miracle of all time.

We've been told about it since we were very young. We've read about it almost since we learned to read. Imagine seeing it for the first time, without knowing that God could even do such a thing? That's the situation of the Israelites. They didn't know that their God had power to open up a Red Sea; but here they saw it with their own eyes for the first time in history! Imagine! God used His power on behalf of a group of slaves.

B. What was their response?

1. They "feared the Lord" (14:31, KJV, RSV, NIV). Who wouldn't be afraid in the presence of such awesome power? After all, they knew their own sinful and rebellious hearts. Just as the power had been used for them, it could be used against them. That's scary!
2. They "revered the Lord" (LB). Their new knowledge of God gave them a new respect for who God was and what He could do. Isn't that always true? The more we know about God through the Bible and personal experience, the more we respect Him.
3. "They stood in awe of the Lord" (TEV).

   Can't you see it? The Israelites were standing on the shore—men, women, and children—with their eyes transfixed on the sea that had just let them cross and had swallowed up the whole mighty army of Egypt. Can you see it? What kind of God is this? AWESOME doesn't describe the epic event, but it captures the emotional tone in a word.
4. "They believed the Lord" (KJV, RSV, LB).

Isn't this the response God wants, the inspiring of faith? It seems that God uses His power to show love, to inspire faith, or to reward faith. Faith pleases God (Hebrews 11:6) and seems to open up unlimited possibilities (Matthew 17:20).

On the other hand, the lack of faith seems (in a way) to tie the Lord's hands. Jesus could not do mighty works in Canaan because of their unbelief, except lay His hands on a few sick people and heal them (Matthew 13:58; Luke 4:23-28).

It is true that the Israelites' burst of faith was temporary. Not too long afterwards, they were complaining about bread and water. But, at least, for a brief moment, they believed God and their faith took them to the next crisis. We understand this, don't we? We have the whole Bible, including the Red Sea episode and almost 2,000 years of church history, and sometimes we still have difficulty believing God for the rent, the mortgage, the car payment, or the salvation of a loved one, don't we?

5. They believed "his servant Moses" (Exodus 14:31). Moses was to the Israelites what Jesus is to the Christians. To them, Moses was the visible presence of God. To hear and obey Moses, was to hear and obey God. At that point, to offend Moses was to offend God. To put their trust (NIV) in God was to put their trust in Moses, also.

   From our Christian vantage point, there's something very scary and very challenging about that statement. It is scary because we know that there are people who are likely to see us in the same light as the Israelites saw Moses. To them, we represent God. We are God's ambassadors, His representatives (2 Corinthians 5:20). The only God some people see is what they see in us. It's scary, because we know about our own deceitful hearts and sinful natures. And we know that we can never measure up to such a God-like perception.

On the other hand, we are challenged because we know we have been sent out into the world (John 20:21) to be exactly what people believe we're supposed to be—the body of Christ—His visible representatives on earth. With fear and trembling, we humbly try to live up to our calling (Ephesians 4:1-2), while pointing people away from ourselves to Christ, who is God's perfect representative.

Daily, we go up to the mountain in prayer and there meditate on His Word. By being with Him, we hope to become more like Him, and to have something to bring down from the mountain that will benefit those to whom we minister. Perhaps when we come to the end of our days, we will receive the historian's highest compliment—the people believed God and (our names), His servants.

DISCERNING MY DUTY

1. *When God is working for human beings, why does He always seem to need a human partner?*
2. *How important was Moses' part in the liberation of Israel from Egypt?*
3. *Would the Israelite slaves have followed God without Moses being present?*

4. *Could African Americans have won their civil rights without Dr. King demonstrating in the streets and having the assistance of the Kennedys and Johnsons presiding in the White House?*
5. *What part did God play in the success of the Civil Rights Movement? Could we have "overcome," had God not been "on our side?"*
6. *What is our part in our salvation, our spiritual liberation from the penalty and power of sin? (See John 1:11-12; 3:16, 36; Romans 1:16; 10:9-10; 1 John 1:9.)*

DECIDING MY RESPONSE

Many of our inner-city public schools are like the Red Sea and many of our children are drowning. Appoint a small committee to investigate the school closest to your church: 1) Discover what the major problems are. 2) Return and discuss what the class (and church) can do to help. 3) Then do it!

LIGHT ON THE HEAVY

PHARAOH. Pharaoh [fay'ro] was a title used as a name, or part of a name, of the kings of ancient Egypt. Among the most important Pharaohs mentioned in the Bible:

1. The Pharaoh whose dream was interpreted by Joseph and who promoted him to a position in the kingdom second only to the Pharaoh himself (Genesis 41:14-41).
2. The Pharaoh under whom the Israelites were forced to work, under oppressive conditions, on the store cities of Pithom and Rameses. It is quite possible that this work was carried on during the reigns of several Pharaohs, namely

Ramses I, Sethos, and Ramses II, the latter of whom was probably ruling at the time of the Exodus (Exodus 1–15).

3. Pharaoh Necho II (609-594 B.C.): Shortly after his accession to the throne, Necho set about to enlarge Egyptian holdings. He met resistance from Josiah, king of Judah and slew that great reformer.
4. Pharaoh Hophra (588-569 B.C.): This ruler invited Zedekiah to revolt against Babylon, thus precipitating the final downfall of Judah in 586 B.C. (William Martin, "Pharaoh," Layman's Bible Encyclopedia, 1964, pp. 608-609).

Bread from Heaven

Based on Exodus 16:2-18

DEFINING THE ISSUE

Some time ago a devastating flood in the Midwest caused tremendous pain and heartache for many people who lived near the Mississippi and Missouri Rivers. Well over 1,000,000 acres of farmland was destroyed. In addition, hundreds of homes were flooded beyond repair. The resources of Illinois, Missouri, Wisconsin, Minnesota, Kansas, Iowa, South Dakota, North Dakota, and Nebraska were stretched to the limit as government officials tried to deal with the problems and turmoil that the flooding caused.

However, organizations such as the Red Cross, World Vision, New Life Evangelistic Center, the Salvation Army, and other social relief agencies provided much needed help to hundreds of thousands of people. Said one lady whose home was literally torn from its foundation by the Missouri River, "I never knew that there were people who cared enough to provide for those who are hurting."

At one time or another, people need some type of provision from a relief agency or social organization that can help during times of stress and turmoil. It is wonderful to know that we can pick up our telephone and get the help we need from those who care.

The Children of Israel weren't able to pick up a telephone and get the help they needed, but they had their intercessor Moses, who was able to call on the Lord, who provided His children with bread from heaven.

AIM

By the end of the lesson, students will be able to retell the story of God providing manna for His people in the wilderness, give specific evidence of how God provides for their needs, and participate in a class project that provides for the needs of others.

SCRIPTURE TEXT

> EXODUS 16:2 And the whole congregation of the children of Israel murmured against Moses and Aaron in the wilderness:
>
> 3 And the children of Israel said unto them, Would to God we had died by the hand of the Lord in the land of Egypt, when we sat by the flesh pots, and when we did eat bread to the full; for ye have brought us forth into this wilderness, to kill this whole assembly with hunger.
>
> 4 Then said the Lord unto Moses, Behold, I will rain bread from heaven for you; and the people shall go out and gather a certain rate every day, that I may prove them, whether they will walk in my law, or no.
>
> 5 And it shall come to pass, that on the sixth day they shall prepare that which they bring in; and it shall be twice as much as they gather daily.

6 And Moses and Aaron said unto all the children of Israel, At even, then ye shall know that the Lord hath brought you out from the land of Egypt:

7 And in the morning, then ye shall see the glory of the Lord; for that he heareth your murmurings against the Lord: and what are we, that ye murmur against us?

13 And it came to pass, that at even the quails came up, and covered the camp: and in the morning the dew lay round about the host.

14 And when the dew that lay was gone up, behold, upon the face of the wilderness there lay a small round thing, as small as the hoar frost on the ground.

15 And when the children of Israel saw it, they said one to another, It is manna: for they wist not what it was. And Moses said unto them, This is the bread which the Lord hath given you to eat.

16 This is the thing which the Lord hath commanded, Gather of it every man according to his eating, an omer for every man, according to the number of your persons; take ye every man for them which are in his tents.

17 And the children of Israel did so, and gathered, some more, some less.

18 And when they did mete it with an omer, he that gathered much had nothing over, and he that gathered little had no lack; they gathered every man according to his eating.

BIBLE BACKGROUND

Israel was a rebellious nation. Following their exodus from Egypt, Moses led the people across the Red Sea into the wilderness on their way to the Promised Land. Yet many of the people either had short memories or could not believe that God was able to protect them (see Exodus 14:12-13).

Once Pharaoh's men drowned in the Red Sea and the Children of Israel walked on dry land, they sang a song of deliverance which is commonly referred to as the "Song of Moses" (Exodus 15:1-19).

Despite God's miraculous intervention and His promise that they would make it to the Promised Land, the Children of Israel complained to Moses that they had no water. God, therefore, told Moses to cast a tree into the bitter water of Marah so that the water might turn sweet and drinkable (15:23-25).

In fact, when the Children of Israel came to Elim, which is about seven miles south of Marah, they found 12 wells of water and 70 palm trees, enough provision to last them quite a while. But the Children of Israel complained once again.

POINTS TO PONDER

1. *Where were the Children of Israel when they began to murmur? (Exodus 16:2)*

   ____

   ____

   ____

2. *What was their main complaint? (v. 3)*

   ____

   ____

   ____

3. *Why did the Lord promise to "rain bread from heaven?" (v. 4)*

___

___

___

4. *Who were the Children of Israel murmuring against? (v. 7)*

___

___

___

5. *What did the people find when they woke up in the morning? (v. 15)*

___

___

___

6. *What commandment did the Lord give the people? (v. 16)*

___

___

___

LESSON AT-A-GLANCE

1. *The Children of Israel murmur for bread (Exodus 16:2-7)*
2. *The Lord of heaven provides bread (vv. 13-18)*

EXPLORING THE MEANING

1. The Children of Israel murmur for bread (Exodus 16:2-7)
According to Charles Ryrie, the Children of Israel had been out of Egypt approximately one month when they arrived in the Wilderness of Sin, which is between Elim and the Sinai desert. They had been blessed by God with enough water to keep them satisfied

while they made their journey across the desert (*Ryrie Study Bible*, 1984, Moody Press, p. 115). However, it was not long before the Children of Israel began to complain, not against Moses and Aaron, but against God. Moses and Aaron were probably fed up with the people, having heard their murmuring and complaints several times.

Not only had they complained about the lack of water, they also complained that they didn't have meat and bread. In fact, their biggest complaint was that they had eaten satisfactorily while in Egypt. Now they had been brought into the wilderness where they assumed that the Lord had brought them to die from starvation! It is true that the Israelites ate quite well while in Egypt (Numbers 11:5). But, to accuse the Lord of trying to murder His own people is absurd!

The biggest problem was that the Israelites lacked faith that God would provide for their needs as well as lead them safely to the Promised Land. Are there people in the church like the Israelites? Do we fail to recognize God's past provisions in our lives? Are we unsure that He will continue to provide for us? Do we question what the Lord is doing in our lives and wonder whether or not He will keep His promises to us? The Scriptures tell us that the Lord is the same yesterday as He is today and as He will be forever (Hebrews 13:8). Certainly, if the Lord makes a promise to us He will keep it!

Perhaps the Lord was angry with the Children of Israel and tired of their complaining. So, God told Moses and Aaron that He was going to "rain bread from heaven" upon His people (Exodus 16:4). Not only was He going to create a miracle for the people, but God's plan was to test them by making sure they only gathered a certain portion of bread every day. In fact, *The Amplified Bible* states that the people "shall go out and gather a day's portion every day" (v. 4). God wanted to teach the people obedience to His Word and what better way to do so than with bread, something they said they wanted so badly.

In addition to giving the people what they wanted, the Lord instructed them to prepare the bread that they brought in and somehow it would be doubled in their camp. When the Lord is in our plans, He knows how to stretch our resources and supply whatever we need.

Moses and Aaron went to the people to report the things that the Lord had told them, and to prove to them that it was God and not anyone else who brought them out of Egypt. The Lord would show His glory to the people by providing for them more than they could possibly eat or need. Moses and Aaron made it clear that their complaining was not against them but the Lord (v. 7). Isn't that one of our biggest problems? We may complain against the pastor, or the church programs, or about those who hold leadership positions in politics, but ultimately our complaint is against the Lord, isn't it?

2. The Lord of heaven provides bread (vv. 13-18)

God's glory cloud came upon the people in the wilderness (v. 10) and He spoke to Moses, telling him that the people would receive quail meat at night and bread in the day. Quails are short-winged, bullet-headed birds that were considered a delicacy in the ancient Near East.

In the morning, dew surrounded the camp. Once the dew lifted, the people saw a "small round substance, as fine as frost on the ground" (v. 14). It must have seemed strange to the people, something they had not seen before, because they asked one another, "What is it?" The Hebrew term for their question is *manna* (*The Amplified Bible*, 1987, p. 87). But Moses was quick to reply to the people, "This is the bread which the Lord has given you to eat" (v. 15). Isn't it interesting that sometimes we ask the Lord for what we want only to be dissatisfied with His reply? The Lord has heard enough complaints from His people. Instead of complaining, shouldn't we be thankful that God has heard our prayers, and is willing to answer them according to His perfect will?

Moses begins to lay out God's feeding program to the people. Every man was to gather enough manna according to his family needs, which the Scriptures says was an *omer*—approximately two quarts. Some people gathered more, some gathered less. Nevertheless, no one went away empty. Everyone went to their tent with enough manna to provide for their needs.

Why should we worry about the future when we know that God is in control? After all, "the Lord is able to supply all of our needs according to His riches in glory by Christ Jesus" (Philippians 4:19).

DISCERNING MY DUTY

1. *Jesus affirmed that He is the Bread from heaven (John 6).*
2. *How do we know that God will provide our needs during difficult circumstances? Give an example of His provision in your life.*
3. *Is it ever appropriate to complain about what God is doing in our lives?*
4. *Does God always provide our needs? Why or why not?*
5. *What specific events in God's provision for the people remind us of an attribute of Jesus Christ?*
6. *Social agencies are working desperately to provide for the needs of homeless and hurting people. Some of these agencies*

are in need of financial help as well as volunteer support. What specific expertise do you have that can be an asset to these agencies in your community? How can the love of Jesus Christ be shown through your help to others?

DECIDING MY RESPONSE

This week, write down your needs that you wish for the Lord to provide. Then, spend time thanking the Lord that He has already met those needs. Be sure to keep a journal in which you record the answer to your prayers.

LIGHT ON THE HEAVY

MANNA. This is a masculine Hebrew noun which literally means "What is it?" For about 40 years, while wandering in the wilderness, manna was the basic food which God provided to the Israelites. He also gave them water and quail. Manna was "bread" from God (Exodus 16:15), "food from heaven" (Psalm 78:24), and "angel's food" (Psalm 78:25, KJV). Manna could be ground or milled, baked or boiled (Exodus 16:23; Numbers 11:8). It was God's miraculous provision for the nation of Israel, not some natural edible substance which happened to grow in the Sinai Peninsula. Only the small portion which Aaron put in the tabernacle remained after the 40-year period.

God taught the people to depend upon Him for their lives (Deuteronomy 8:3). Jesus made it clear that man could not live by manna alone when He met the devil in the wilderness (Matthew 4:4; Luke 4:4). Jesus, Himself, is the true manna (John 6). (*The Hebrew-Greek Key Study Bible*, Compiled and Edited by Spiros Zodhiates, Nashville: World Bible Publishers, Inc., 1991, p. 1629)

A Covenant to Keep

Based on Exodus 19:1-20:17

DEFINING THE ISSUE

The room was thick and tense with silence. A dozen people sat in folding chairs, nervous, tired, and . . . hopeful. These were drug addicts who had heard the Gospel through Urbanline, a group of Christian ex-addicts who shared Christ with addicts on the street. The program was tough. Michael Johnson, the director, explained the program to the group.

"We have a 90% success rate here at Urbanline. That's because we recognize that the best way to deal with an addiction is to replace it with the ultimate addiction: Jesus Christ. The Lord Jesus Christ will become your "fix." Television viewing is monitored so that there is no temptation through the images portrayed. Every day is Sunday . . . we start the day with Bible study and prayer. We are praying for you and with you all day, and we end the day with Bible study and prayer. Old habits like lying, stealing, accusing each other will go out the window. These were tactics for getting drugs. Some of you even used your wives, girlfriends, and children to supply your habits." Heads hung low.

"You have made a commitment to Jesus Christ . . . a covenant . . . that involves your life. You were slaves to powders and crystals. Christ has set you free. But even freedom has conditions. There are things you must do to stay free. If anyone has a problem with any of this, he is free to go." There were sighs and shuffling of feet. Tears stung the eyes of Carl Smith as he fought to keep from running out of the room.

Michael continued, "I suppose the question is, will you be a slave to drugs or a son of the King?" Carl relaxed and wiped the tears away. He would be the son of the King.

AIM

By the end of the lesson, participants will become more familiar with the Ten Commandments, a covenant summed up by our Lord Jesus Christ in two new commandments: love God and love your neighbor. Students will also use the coming week as Ten Commandments' Awareness Week, taking note of two things:

> 1) how well they keep the commandments; 2) watch and read the news, noticing how our society is affected by the keeping or breaking of the Ten Commandments.

SCRIPTURE TEXT

> EXODUS 19:4 Ye have seen what I did unto the Egyptians, and how I bare you on eagles' wings, and brought you unto myself.
>
> 5 Now therefore, if ye will obey my voice indeed, and keep my covenant, then ye shall be a peculiar treasure unto me above all people: for all the earth is mine:
>
> 6 And ye shall be unto me a kingdom of priests, and a holy nation. These are the words which thou shalt speak unto the children of Israel.

20:2 I am the Lord thy God, which have brought thee out of the land of Egypt, out of the house of bondage.

3 Thou shalt have no other gods before me.

4 Thou shalt not make unto thee any graven image, or any likeness of any thing that is in heaven above, or that is in the earth beneath, or that is in the water under the earth:

7 Thou shalt not take the name of the Lord thy God in vain; for the Lord will not hold him guiltless that taketh his name in vain.

8 Remember the sabbath day, to keep it holy.

9 Six days shalt thou labour, and do all thy work:

10 But the seventh day is the sabbath of the Lord thy God: in it thou shalt not do any work, thou, nor thy son, nor thy daughter, thy manservant, nor thy maidservant, nor thy cattle, nor thy stranger that is within thy gates:

11 For in six days the Lord made heaven and earth, the sea, and all that in them is, and rested the seventh day: wherefore the Lord blessed the Sabbath day, and hallowed it.

12 Honour thy father and thy mother: that thy days may be long upon the land which the Lord thy God giveth thee.

13 Thou shalt not kill.

14 Thou shalt not commit adultery.

15 Thou shalt not steal.

16 Thou shalt not bear false witness against thy neighbour.

17 Thou shalt not covet thy neighbour's house, thou shalt not covet thy neighbour's wife, nor his manservant, nor his maidservant, nor his ox, nor his ass, nor any thing that is thy neighbour's.

BIBLE BACKGROUND

The Hebrews had been free from their Egyptian slave masters for roughly three months. They were encamped in the Sinai desert in front of Mount Horeb. Moses had gone up the mountain at God's command to receive instructions for these people who were destined to be God's special treasure.

The laws received by Moses for the Hebrews would accomplish three basic things: reverse the effects of slavery; nullify the impact of 430 years of Egyptian religion, customs, traditions, and government; and, prepare the people to be a unique nation whose King would be God.

The most memorable of all the laws and ordinances are what we know as the "Ten Commandments," the last six upon which hang the justice systems of many of the civilized countries in the world.

POINTS TO PONDER

1. *Which three commandments defined God's relationship with His people? (Exodus 20:3-7)*

   ____

   ____

   ____

2. *What two things did God do to the Sabbath? (20:11)*

____

____

____

3. *Which six commandments define our relationships with each other? (20:12-17)*

____

____

____

4. *Which commandment had a promise attached? (20:12)*

____

____

____

5. *List six specific things we should not covet. (20:17)*

____

____

____

LESSON AT-A-GLANCE

1. *The God of the Covenant (Exodus 19:4)*
2. *The people of the Covenant (19:5)*
3. *The goal of the Covenant (19:6)*
4. *The Covenant (20:2-17)*
   A. *With respect to God—the fear clause (20:2-7)*
   B. *With respect to self—the faith clause (20:8-11)*
   C. *With respect to each other—the love clause (20:12-17)*

EXPLORING THE MEANING

1. The God of the Covenant (Exodus 19:4)
With the phrase, "Ye have seen what I did unto the Egyptians," God announces Himself to be the exclusive God of the people of Israel. With miracles worked through His awesome power, God not only freed the Israelites, He brought judgment on the gods of the Egyptians. Each plague was an attack on an Egyptian deity. This was an easy thing to do, since the Egyptians worshiped almost everything. He had proven Himself infinitely more powerful than their magic or gods.

His method of deliverance and this reminder was necessary as God set about to undo 430 years of Egyptian culture (religion, politics, economics), as well as to reverse the effects of slavery, including fear of failure and dependence on an oppressor. He required their undivided loyalty and gave them a religion (Judaism), government (theocracy), and an economic system (giving and forgiving).

2. The people of the Covenant (19:5)
God gave the people one basic stipulation: Obey. He does not require that they do great feats, go beyond their capabilities, or make unreasonable sacrifices. He simply insists that they obey His voice. Why? If they were not willing to obey His voice, how would He provide for them, protect them, lead and bless them? These benefits were all a part of the covenant—His agreement with them.

The Christian liberty we enjoy in Christ Jesus as an integral part of the New Covenant also involves our obedience. If we do not obey the Word of God, not only do we suffer the natural and spiritual consequences of disobedience, but our salvation may be called into question. The kind of life we lead is a reflection of the level of our commitment to Christ and His New Covenant.

3. The goal of the Covenant (19:6)

The goal of the covenant was to make Israel a nation unlike any other nation, a nation whose King was God—a theocracy. Their nation was not to be one whose religion was based on shedding the blood of its people in sacrifices to its god, or whose economic stability and prosperity was based on preying on other nations. Their system of giving tithes and offerings would ensure that everyone was taken care of. The forgiving of their sins and debts, and the receiving of the abundant blessings from their God, were the benefits they would receive for obeying and honoring the covenant.

4. The Covenant (20:2-17)

A. *With respect to God—the fear clause (20:2-7)*

The first three commandments would ensure that the people of Israel's religion would be different from other nations.

They were prohibited from worshiping any other gods. Other nations had few problems with "mixing and matching" gods. Other nations often worshiped many gods. In Egypt, for example, almost everything in nature was worshiped as a god—even flies! The Hebrews would worship ONE God, proven greater than all the others (vv. 3-4).

Further, they would not be allowed to create images of their God. To do so would reduce Him from His rightfully exalted position. Images would confine God, who is Spirit, to space and eventually confine Him to their own perceptions and private interpretations of Him. If a physical image of God could be formed by their own imaginations and hands, sooner or later, they would do the same to the very character and nature of God, distorting Him and reducing Him to a deity who could be carved, fashioned, and manipulated. Further down the road, they might convince themselves that He had given permission to practice the perversions of other cultures. They are reminded by this command that God alone is the Creator and they are the creatures.

He informs them that He is a jealous God and the consequences of His jealousy, confronted by disobedience to these commands, would be felt to the third and fourth generations of those who despise Him by doing things contrary to His laws. On the other hand, He would show mercy to those who love and obey Him.

Finally, even His Name must be reverenced. Others, frequently without thought, invoked the names of their gods in even the most trivial matters of conversation. This would not be so in Israel.

These three commandments can be called the "fear clause," a reminder that they have an awesome God, who is to be reverenced and His authority respected and unchallenged.

B. *With respect to self—the faith clause (20:8-11)*

Of the seven days of the week, one day was to be a day of rest from all labor. God initiated this day of rest when He rested or stood back from His own works (Genesis 2:2-3).

What was the purpose and benefits of the Sabbath? First, there was the obvious need to rest physically, so that the body could be refreshed and renewed. The Lord wanted the Israelites to be a robust and vigorous people. Second, slaves do not have "off days." They are on duty at all times. The Israelites were no longer slaves. This day of rest would be one of God's methods of reversing the effects of slavery. Only the free could afford time off.

Next, the Sabbath would serve as a reminder of their dependence on God, who had provided for them and continued to do so, even as they rested from their labors (Exodus 16:22-30). Finally, the Sabbath would provide a day for the people not only to rest, but to reflect upon their God, to be grateful to Him for all He had done, and to come together to worship Him and thank Him for His continuing mercy and blessings.

This was the "faith clause," which encouraged Israel to continue believing in God's ability and willingness to protect and provide. God would provide for them but His doing so would not be based on their own works, but on His grace toward them.

C. *With respect to each other—the love clause (20:12-17)*

The last six commandments of the Covenant are meant to foster unity and community among the people starting with the family. Children are encouraged to honor their parents. This is the only commandment with a promise attached.

The New Testament not only states that long life is promised, but that life would "go well" with obedient children (Ephesians 6:2-3). Of course, this could be taken literally, since there would be laws calling for the stoning of insubordinate children. But the promised blessing was also social and spiritual because an obedient child would most likely become a cooperative, pleasant, law abiding adult.

Murder, the intentional taking of innocent life, is prohibited. Hence, captured in this commandment is the premise that human life is precious. If people are permitted to kill at will, there would soon be no people. We need to give serious thought to the rate at which violence in our "modern and enlightened" society is reducing our population—particularly the young, African American male population.

Adultery is forbidden. Since marriage is a covenant instituted by God, adultery severely damages and/or nullifies that covenant. Adultery not only disrupts the covenant between the marriage partners, but affects family unity, so that it cannot effectively carry out God's plans and purposes.

Stealing was not only wrong but unnecessary in God's "perfect" society where one serves the Lord who provides for His people and blesses them abundantly. To steal would be to imply that God had failed to provide for His own. This would be the opinion of the outsider looking in on God's people. The truth is that stealing would merely expose one's own innate greed, ingratitude, and discontent with what God has provided. It also shows an attitude of not caring for one's neighbor and not respecting that neighbor's possessions.

Lying to and on each other is one sure way to disrupt the unity of community life. Since trust in any context is based on truth, when truth is absent, trust becomes impossible. When one cannot trust one's neighbor, suspicion settles in. If we cannot trust those we see every day because of lies, then how will we fully trust God whom we cannot see? If we lie on each other, what is there to prevent us from lying on or about God?

Finally, *coveting* or the lusting for the possessions of other people or their body is condemned. Those possessing less wealth might be tempted to want what their neighbors have, and unchecked, these intense desires could lead to hostilities and acts of stealing, lying, and even murder.

We, therefore, see that the Ten Commandments are not simply a childhood recitation, but a serious, abiding covenant in 10 parts, designed to shape a meaningful, caring, free society for those who would choose to live by that Covenant. These commandments are God-given, ageless, and timeless—working as well in today's society as in the Israelite camp of over 4,000 years ago.

DISCERNING MY DUTY

1. *Why do you think God started out with just 10 basic laws for His people?*
2. *How could these laws help the Israelites experience a sense of community?*
3. *Why did God begin by reminding the people of what He had done for them?*
4. *What do you think was the significance of the first three commandments? Could God have added other commandments concerning Himself? Give an example.*
5. *How could the last six commandments provide a good foundation, even for a non-Christian society?*

DECIDING MY RESPONSE

Read the Ten Commandments in Exodus 20:3-17. Let's make this Ten Commandments' Awareness Week. Be aware of how well you keep the Ten Commandments. Are you taking the Lord's name in vain ("Oh, Lord! "Jesus Christ!" "Lordy, Lordy!")? While most Christians do not use profanity habitually, sometimes things come out of our mouths which should not, don't they? And, sometimes we wish we could have Brother Rich's BMW. When was the last time your response to a phone call was, "Tell them I'm not in"? Share with the class next week the results of Ten Commandments' Awareness Week—and maybe have a few chuckles as well.

LIGHT ON THE HEAVY

COVENANT. Covenant is not an everyday term in modern society; "contract" is its substitute. What's the difference? In biblical use "covenant" differs from a contract in two ways. First, a covenant has no termination date, whereas a contract always does. Second, a covenant applies to the whole of a person, whereas a contract involves only a part, especially a skill possessed by a person or a service to be rendered. In the Old Testament, the Hebrew word *berith* is translated as covenant, and comes from a root which means "to cut." This refers to the cutting or dividing of animals into two parts and the two parties of the covenant passing between them in making the covenant. (*Dictionary of the Bible*, Carmel, Guideposts)

God's Constant Presence

Based on Exodus 25:1-8; 29:42-46; 40:33-38

DEFINING THE ISSUE

One of the greatest fears we can have as we grow older is that of being abandoned or left alone. One older woman, whom I will call Ruth, shared with me her anxieties of being alone and how she overcame them. She was raised in an extended family and someone was always at their home. She enjoyed coming home. She said to me, "I cannot see how anyone could live by themselves and not have anyone to talk to. I could not live like that." One day the thing she feared most was realized. The last member of her family died, and she had no husband or children. She was suddenly all alone. She was afraid to love another pet, because the last one she had was killed by a car. Ruth had no one to turn to except Jesus. She drew on her Christian experience and prayed until the presence of God became more real than ever. Her favorite hymn was "I Come to the Garden," by C. Austin Miles:

> *"I come to the garden alone while the dew is still on the roses; and the voice I hear,*
>
> *falling on my ear,*
>
> *the son of God discloses . . .*
>
> *And He walks with me,*

and He talks with me,
and He then tells me
I am His own"

In the words of that song, Ruth found assurance that she would never be alone.

We learn in our lesson today that God made specific plans to constantly dwell with His people.

AIM

By the end of the lesson, participants will better understand the structure and beauty of the tabernacle, appreciate its importance to Israel during their desert years, and will actively begin to maintain and improve the health of their bodies—their personal tabernacle. This is God's gift and temporary dwelling place.

SCRIPTURE TEXT

EXODUS 25:1 And the Lord spake unto Moses, saying,

2 Speak unto the children of Israel, that they bring me an offering: of every man that giveth it willingly with his heart ye shall take my offering.

3 And this is the offering which ye shall take of them; gold, and silver, and brass,

4 And blue, and purple, and scarlet, and fine linen, and goats' hair,

5 And rams' skins dyed red, and badgers' skins, and shittim wood,

6 Oil for the light, spices for anointing oil, and for sweet incense,

7 Onyx stones, and stones to be set in the ephod, and in the breastplate.

8 And let them make me a sanctuary; that I may dwell among them.

29:42 This shall be a continual burnt offering throughout your generations at the door of the tabernacle of the congregation before the Lord: where I will meet you, to speak there unto thee.

43 And there I will meet with the children of Israel, and the tabernacle shall be sanctified by my glory.

44 And I will sanctify the tabernacle of the congregation, and the altar: I will sanctify also both Aaron and his sons, to minister to me in the priest's office.

45 And I will dwell among the children of Israel, and will be their God.

46 And they shall know that I am the Lord their God, that brought them forth out of the land of Egypt, that I may dwell among them: I am the Lord their God.

40:33 So Moses finished the work.

34 Then a cloud covered the tent of the congregation, and the glory of the Lord filled the tabernacle.

35 And Moses was not able to enter into the tent of the congregation, because the cloud abode thereon, and the glory of the Lord filled the tabernacle.

36 And when the cloud was taken up from over the tabernacle, the children of Israel went onward in all their journeys:

37 But if the cloud were not taken up, then they journeyed not till the day that it was taken up.

38 For the cloud of the Lord was upon the tabernacle by day, and fire was on it by night, in the sight of all the house of Israel, throughout all their journeys.

BIBLE BACKGROUND

In the great Exodus, God delivered the Israelites from the bondage of the Egyptians, defeated Pharaoh and his army, and established Himself as Israel's God. The people are now encamped at Mount Sinai, about to move on toward Canaan. They have already been given the Law and have a divinely appointed leader. A house that represents God's presence in the midst remains to be built. It will be designed by God and God expects the people to give of their possessions for its construction. The Tabernacle would symbolize God's presence in the midst of His people. Yet it was to be distinct from them, and set apart from them because of His holiness. (H. L. Ellison, *Exodus*, Philadelphia: Westminster Press, 1982, p. 161).

POINTS TO PONDER

1. *Why did God ask for a "freewill" offering and not simply an offering?*

 ____

 ____

 ____

2. *What was the importance of a freewill offering?*

3. *What did the freewill offering consist of?*

4. *What was to be done with it? (Exodus 25:1-8)*

5. *What is the significance of the continual burnt offering at the door of the tabernacle? (29:42-43)*

6. *Why did Aaron and his sons have to be consecrated? (v. 44)*

7. *What promise to the Israelites was instituted in verses 44 and 45?*

8. *What happened when Moses completed the tabernacle? (40:33-34)*

____

____

____

9. *Why was Moses unable to enter the tabernacle? (v. 35)*

____

____

____

10. *What is the importance of the Glory cloud in the wilderness experience of the Israelites? (vv. 36-38)*

____

____

____

LESSON AT-A-GLANCE

1. Moses receives an offering to build the tabernacle (Exodus 25:1-8)
2. The Lord requests daily offerings (29:42-43)
3. God consecrates Aaron and his sons as priests (v. 44)
4. The Lord promises to dwell among the Israelites (vv. 45-46)
5. Moses completes the tabernacle (40:33-38)

EXPLORING THE MEANING

1. Moses receives an offering to build the tabernacle (Exodus 25:1-8)

God speaks to Moses and says, "Tell the Israelites to bring me an offering" (v. 2, NIV), a freewill offering, from each man whose heart prompts him to give. God specified the various items which the people were to bring (vv. 3-7) and later directed how these items were to be used. This was not an impossible task for the people to do, because they had received many precious metals, cloth, and gems from the Egyptians. Acacia trees grew in the area where they were camped. Oil, spices, and incense could be purchased from caravans passing through the area.

The freewill offering was for a sanctuary where the Lord promised to dwell among His people. As noted in our text, the Lord Himself would show Moses a picture or model of the tabernacle and its furniture. (Wendland, Ernst, *Exodus*, St. Louis: Concordia, 1973, p. 173).

2. The Lord requests daily offerings (29:42-43)

In addition to this one-time offering for the building of the tabernacle, there were daily offerings that were to be made at the door of the tabernacle. These signified that Israel was to consecrate their daily life to the Lord. The Lord, in turn, promised He would meet and speak to the Israelites and manifest His glorious presence. The continual offering reminded them of the constant presence of the Lord. At the door, the people could see His glory as they made their animal sacrifices.

In the New Testament, the sacrifice of animals was no longer necessary to recall the presence of God. Today, we live in the presence of the Holy Spirit that dwells within us. Jesus was slain for our justification; we, therefore can go daily to "the throne of grace, that we may obtain mercy, and find grace to help in the time of need" (Hebrews 4:16).

The lamb that was offered every morning and evening typified the continual intercessions which Christ now makes for His church. He offered Himself once and for all, and that one offering becomes a continual offering for us. The daily offerings also teach us to offer to God the spiritual sacrifices of prayer and praise every day, morning and evening. Our daily devotions are the most important of our daily works and the most pleasant of our daily comforts. Prayer time is as important as mealtime. Our spiritual life-needs are to be nourished as are our physical health-needs.

3. God consecrates Aaron and his sons as priests (v. 44)

The consecration sets Aaron and his sons apart from the rest of the community as a sanctified group, to serve in the sacred precincts of the sanctuary and to provide a liaison between God and the people. In the first part of the ritual (vv. 1-9), the initiates are bathed and dressed in the garments described in the preceding chapter. The sacrifice of ordination (vv. 9-37) has three parts. The first animal is a young bull, which is offered as a "sin offering" (v. 14, RSV), or a purifying offering. The sacrifice is not performed for the offerer, but on behalf of the sanctuary, which is purged from pollution. Some of the blood is smeared on the horns of the altar, drawing off the impurity and thus preparing the altar to receive the next sacrifice (30:10).

The second animal is a ram, which is sacrificed as a whole burnt offering (29:18). Its purpose is to be a substitute, and to atone for the sins of the offerer, thus making them eligible for the sanctification of the third sacrifice. The third animal is another ram, ("the ram of ordination") (v. 22, RSV). Just as the blood of the bull was smeared on the horns of the altar, the blood of the second ram is dabbed on the right ear lobe, the right thumb, and the right big toe of the offerer. The blood again draws off the impurities, and the new priests are now sanctified. (*Harper's Bible Dictionary*, New York: Harper and Row, 1988, p. 152)

After the day-to-day offerings of the appointed animal sacrifices, the greatest care was taken to keep the altar properly cleansed—to remove the ashes, and sprinkle them as prescribed, at the conclusion of the ceremony. This was done so that the altar itself would be consecrated as well as the ministers who officiated at it (Matthew 23:19).

The priests were set apart for the service of the Lord. They were cleansed of all of their impurities and sanctified for His service. Should believers do likewise if we desire to work in the service of our Lord? Should we not commit ourselves to Jesus Christ and let Him cleanse us from all unrighteousness? The blood of the animals was symbolic of the cleansing blood of Jesus Christ. The blood that Jesus shed at Calvary cleanses us of our sins and sanctifies us through the truth. As the priests were sanctified and set aside for the service of the Lord, so are we. We may also look at the cleansing of the altar as the cleansing of our hearts. Jeremiah says, "the heart is deceitful . . . and desperately wicked; who can know it?" (Jeremiah 17:9) "For out of the heart proceed evil thoughts, murders, adulteries, fornications, thefts, false witness, blasphemies: These are the things which defile a [person]" (Matthew 15:19, 20). As the altar had to be cleansed properly to remove all defilements, so our hearts must be cleansed likewise.

4. The Lord promises to dwell among Israel (vv. 45-46)

Every morning and every evening, a lamb was to be offered together with a grain offering. These offerings were to be "a pleasing aroma, a food offering presented to the Lord." (Exodus 29:41, NIV). These daily offerings signified that Israel was to consecrate their daily life to the Lord. The Lord, in turn, promised that He would dwell with them (v. 45).

For Israel, serving the Lord was a daily matter. How clearly that morning and evening service should have served to impress upon them the need for a daily rededication to the Lord! The Lord was not only to be remembered in time of a special need, or at special occasions, but His presence among them was never failing. Their sacrifices were a daily expression of their devotion to Him.

Our Christian churches today are not built according to the same Old Testament pattern which the Lord gave to Moses. Yet our churches are symbols of the place where the Lord meets His people. He meets us through His Holy Word and precious sacraments. In most of our churches, our attention is directed to the cross. Before the Lord's altar, the congregation brings all its requests to Him in prayer, and receives the Lord's own body and blood in "the Lord's Supper." We, too, want that place we call our "house of God" to reflect the place where God dwells. (*Matthew Henry Concise Commentary*, Chicago: Moody Press)

5. Moses completes the tabernacle (40:33-38)

"Moses finished the work. Then the cloud covered the tent of meeting, and the glory of the Lord filled the tabernacle" (vv. 33-34, RSV). The construction of the tabernacle is now completed. It has been consecrated and the glory of the Lord filled the place of worship. The separation from common use is effected by anointing with the holy oil. The cloud covering the tabernacle signifies the presence of God according to the promise of Exodus 29:43-45. It also signifies the visible evidence of God's favor. And even though Moses could not enter, God's presence there is symbolized so that

His people may have communion with Him in accord with the appointed means.

How appropriate that the Book of Exodus closes with this final, visible demonstration of the glory of God. "The glory of the Lord filled the tabernacle," to let His people know that here they could find the assurance of forgiveness of their sins, and fellowship with the God who delivered them. Here, their offerings could be brought to atone for their sins, and they could demonstrate their devotion to Him as His kingdom of priests and holy people. They could also give praise and thanksgiving to His Name and find fellowship with their gracious God. They could bring their prayers to His throne of grace. Here, He dwelt among them as their God, and they as His people.

DISCERNING MY DUTY

1. *God had Moses erect a tabernacle in the wilderness. Why was the tabernacle important?*
2. *God asked for a freewill offering of precious metals to build the tabernacle. Why was the material offering important? Do we overdo the decoration of our churches today?*
3. *God asked for a continual burnt offering at the door of the tabernacle. What kinds of continual offering does God expect of us as New Testament believers?*
4. *God's presence dwelled with the Israelites to demonstrate to them that He was the God that brought them out of the land of Egypt. What does the indwelling of the Holy Spirit remind us of?*
5. *How does God demonstrate His presence in our society today?*
6. *What has taken the place of the tabernacle in the world today?*

7. *In what ways can society see the presence of the Lord in the church?*
8. *In addition to the church, are the NAACP, Red Cross, Cancer Society, and the United Nations symbols of God's presence in the world?*

DECIDING MY RESPONSE

God is everywhere, but it is through our bodies that He most vividly demonstrates His love. How long has it been since your body (your tabernacle) has had a maintenance check? This week, make an appointment to see your doctor for a check-up of your eyes, ears, blood pressure, cholesterol, and sugar levels. Urge your classmates to join you.

LIGHT ON THE HEAVY

EPHOD. The *ephod* was one of the eight garments worn by the high priest. It was loose-fitting and worn over a blue tunic secured by two shoulder straps and a belt around the middle (Exodus 28:31). The shoulder straps bore two precious onyx stones engraved with the names of the 12 sons of Jacob, six on each stone (28:5-14). The front of the ephod carried the breastplate with the Urim and Thummim [two objects which stood for "yes" and "no" which the high priest used as symbols for making decisions (Exodus 28:30)]. Occasionally, the term *ephod* referred to the garment, together with the breastplate and the Urim and Thummim. It is believed that consultation through the Urim and Thummim discontinued as early as the First Temple period, but the high priest continued to wear the ephod throughout the annals of both Temple periods.

The ephod was made of blue, purple, and scarlet fine linen, with strands of gold thread from the tabernacle curtains and veil of the Ark (Exodus 39:2-3). It thus helped to symbolize the close relationship of the high priest to the tabernacle and the Holy of Holies. (Wigoder, Geoffrey, et al., *Illustrated Dictionary of the Bible*, Jerusalem: Jerusalem Publishing House, 1986, p. 324; The *Interpreter's Dictionary of the Bible*, Nashville: Abingdon Press, 1962, p. 118) (Alan Richardson, editor, *A Theological Word Book of the Bible*, New York: MacMillan, 1950, p. 174)

A Celebration of Justice

Based on Leviticus 25:8-12, 25-28, 39-42

DEFINING THE ISSUE

The year 1986 was the first year for the annual national celebration of the life of Reverend Dr. Martin Luther King, Jr., "Drum Major for Justice!" Many insightful Black historians and social activists pointed out the hypocrisies of many Whites and "flunky" Blacks, who disdained, well-nigh hated, Dr. King and his principles during his lifetime, but now were embellishing his "tomb" with sanctimonious platitudes. Celebration was now safe, since the prophet was now dead!

So concerned was the covenant-God of Israel about alleviating social inequities and oppressions that He institutionalized a system of correction. This system was called the *Jubilee,* and was intended to be a *celebration of justice.*

AIM

By the end of the study, participants will understand the meaning and purpose of Jubilee, will identify with God's motive of justice for the poor in establishing it, and will become concerned for justice in our day.

SCRIPTURE TEXT

LEVITICUS 25:8 And thou shalt number seven sabbaths of years unto thee, seven times seven years; and the space of the seven sabbaths of years shall be unto thee forty and nine years.

9 Then shalt thou cause the trumpet of the jubilee to sound on the tenth day of the seventh month, in the day of atonement shall ye make the trumpet sound throughout all your land.

10 And ye shall hallow the fiftieth year, and proclaim liberty throughout all the land unto all the inhabitants thereof: it shall be a jubilee unto you; and ye shall return every man unto his possession, and ye shall return every man unto his family.

11 A jubliee shall that fiftieth year be unto you: ye shall not sow, neither reap that which groweth of itself in it, nor gather the grapes in it of thy vine undressed.

12 For it is the jubilee; it shall be holy unto you: ye shall eat the increase thereof out of the field.

25:25 If thy brother be waxen poor, and hath sold away some of his possession, and if any of his kin come to redeem it, then shall he redeem that which his brother sold.

26 And if the man have none to redeem it, and himself be able to redeem it;

27 Then let him count the years of the sale thereof, and restore the overplus unto the man to whom he sold it; that he may return unto his possession.

28 But if he be not able to restore it to him, then that which is sold shall remain in the hand of him that hath bought it until the year of jubilee: and in the jubilee it shall go out, and he shall return unto his possession.

25:39 And if thy brother that dwelleth by thee be waxen poor, and be sold unto thee; thou shalt not compel him to serve as a bondservant:

40 But as a hired servant, and as a sojourner, he shall be with thee, and shall serve thee unto the year of jubilee:

41 And then shall he depart from thee, both he and his children with him, and shall return unto his own family, and unto the possession of his fathers shall he return.

42 For they are my servants, which I brought forth out of the land of Egypt: they shall not be sold as bondmen.

BIBLE BACKGROUND

Leviticus 25:1-7 records the Sabbatic year and verses 8-55 record the Jubilee year, which served as a climactic year to seven Sabbatic years. Thus, the year of Jubilee occurred every fiftieth (50th) year (Leviticus 25:10).

The Jubilee year was characterized by restoration and liberation. The land was completely left to rest (as in the Sabbatic year). Land that had been alienated was restored to its original owners. Land value was newly appraised and God miraculously provided bumper crops and safety. All Jews, who through poverty had become indentured servants, were now released from bondage.

POINTS TO PONDER

1. *On which day was the trumpet signaling the Jubilee to be sounded? (Leviticus 25:9)*

___

___

___

2. *To what and to whom was each man to return during the year of Jubilee? (25:10)*

___

___

___

3. *The Jubilee was especially established to aid what class of people? (25:25)*

___

___

___

4. *If a man or his family were too poor to redeem land, what was the final resort? (25:28)*

___

___

___

5. *How were the Israelites to treat their fellow Israelites who sold themselves for survival purposes? (vv. 39, 40)*

___

___

___

6. *What did slavery in Egypt have to do with the Jubilee? (25:42)*

____

____

____

LESSON AT-A-GLANCE

1. *The consecration of the Jubilee (Leviticus 25:8-12)*
2. *The justice of the Jubilee (25:25-28, 39-42)*
   A. *Geo-economic justice (25:25-28)*
   B. *Personal and familial justice (25:39-42)*

EXPLORING THE MEANING

1. The consecration of the Jubilee (Leviticus 25:8-12)

Jubilee was to be nation-wide and legal. It was instituted as such by God in His law and was enforceable through the religious/civil authorities.

The Lord understood the sinful nature, even among His covenant people. There were some things whose very nature necessitated that they adopt a legal core. Justice would, otherwise, not be done. This should be a word to the wise concerning attempts to abolish the Voting Rights Act and affirmative action laws and quotas. The policies and attempts of certain politicians to cast the poor and unemployed upon the mercy of the corporate structure in a "trickle-down" theory of economics overlook an important consideration. People are greedy and selfish. Laws are needed to protect the rights of the poor, powerless, and oppressed.

As a legalized national observance, Jubilee was to be regarded as a consecrated occasion ("hallow," v. 10). Since the children of

Israel were a "holy nation" (Exodus 19:6), this holiness was to be demonstrated in everything they did, including liberating the oppressed and less fortunate. Justice is sacred. It is more than the provision of a humane society. Today, He shows us His mercy because His Son atoned for our sin on the cross. Justice flows from the very nature of God. The holiness of God demands that He do justly. In this light, the year of Jubilee was to be regarded just as sacred, just as spiritual an observance, as the day of Atonement.

Of this festival-year God said, "It is a jubilee and it is to be *holy for you*" (25:12, NIV).

But, alas! Of all the festivals instituted by God, there is not a single clear reference to the enforcement of the Jubilee in all the Old Testament. The nation of Israel seemed to have dropped Jubilee cold. They may have been for "justice," but in no way were they promotive of the systemic justice demanded in the Jubilee.

It is obvious that Israel's neglect and denial of systemic justice parallels the treatment of Black and Native Americans in this country as well as numerous other people groups around the world. There is inadequate national justice.

2. The justice of the Jubilee (25:25-28, 39-42)

Laws of justice dealing with three kinds of property are given in the 25th chapter of Leviticus. Property *in land* is covered in verses 13-28. Property *in houses* is covered in verses 29-34. And, slaves *as property* is covered in verses 35-55.

A. *Geo-economic justice (25:25-28)*

When they entered the land of Canaan, each of the 12 tribes of Israel received allotments of land as an inheritance (cf. The book of Joshua). The land was further divided, subdivided, and parceled to families and households.

In the course of time, some of the heads of the households would become poor (perhaps due to a series of crop failures in an agrarian society). In order to survive, a man would sell some of his property and vacate the premises. Since, in every society, there are usually more poor and less fortunate people than other people, the possibility existed that a few powerful families could acquire vast amounts of land. This would lead to oppression, exploitation, and a lopsided political advantage.

To break the power and trim the fortunes of the few, God established a means whereby those who had sold their property could have it redeemed and restored to its original family. There were three possibilities. (1) A near relative could redeem the property (25:25). (2) The man who sold it could experience a turn of circumstances which afforded him the opportunity to redeem his property, provided he pay a prorated amount valued according to the years remaining to the coming Jubilee (25:26-27). (3) When all else failed, the buyer of the land was required to return the land to its original inheritors, receiving no financial remuneration, when the next Jubilee arrived (25:28).

Thus, every fifty years the economic flow of the nation, relative to land holdings, would reach some sense of parity.

B. *Personal and familial justice (25:39-42)*

Some heads of households would resort to selling themselves into slavery when there were no other alternatives. At least they would be provided with shelter and food by their masters. The potential for human abuse occurring within such a system is apparent. Holding people as property is degenerating and dangerous to a civil society.

God gave laws to protect the slave. (1) The person who sold himself into slavery must not be forced to work as a slave. Instead, his owner was to relate to him as a "hired worker" or a "temporary resident" (25:39, 42). (2) The indentured servant was only required to work until the next Jubilee, at which time he and his children were to be released, so they could return to their own family and property (vv. 40-41). (3) The dynamic driving the people of Israel to honor these laws was a remembrance of their status as former slaves in the land of Egypt, and "the fear of God" (vv. 42-43).

Thus, every fifty years each man regained the potential of becoming self-supporting once again, and of carrying on his family life. He would be free.

Any good reading of passages such as Leviticus chapter 25, highlights all the more the godless and desecrating form of slavery experienced by Blacks at the hands of White America. This nation needs to pray to God for forgiveness for the sins of slavery, make restitution to kindred of former slaves, and enact just and righteous laws that are promotive of freedom and self-determination. Jubilee should be proclaimed!

DISCERNING MY DUTY

1. *What effect would the laws of the Jubilee, occurring every 50 years, have on the economy of a nation?*
2. *Why is the administration of justice for the poor and varied ethnic groups in a country so difficult?*
3. *Why is the equal distribution of land so important to God, to people?*

4. *How could White slave masters perpetuate American slavery when they read about the liberating laws of the Jubilee in the Book of Leviticus?*
5. *Should America now atone for the enslavement of Blacks 200 years ago? If so, in what ways might atonement be made?*

DECIDING MY RESPONSE

Current policies of the public welfare system reward families which do not have fathers living in the household. We know this is destructive of the Black family. It is especially unjust and desecrating to God's creation. In your church, consider starting a letter-writing campaign to your governmental representatives and legislators to change these socially defeating policies.

Also, do a comparison study of slavery mentioned in the Bible and North American slavery. Note the similarities and differences.

LIGHT ON THE HEAVY

JUBILEE. Three essential features characterized Jubilee. (1) Liberty was to be proclaimed to all Israelites who were in bondage to any of their countrymen. (2) There was to be a return of ancestral possessions to those who had been compelled to sell them because of poverty. (3) The year was to be a time of rest for the land. The land was to be allowed to stand fallow, as people lived meagerly off what had grown of itself in the sixth year. It is unknown whether or not Jubilee was ever observed. (*The Zondervan Pictorial Bible Dictionary*, Zondervan Publishing, Grand Rapids, MI, pp. 452, 453)

Obey and Be Blessed

Based on Exodus 40:1-9; Leviticus 26:2-6, 11-13

DEFINING THE ISSUE

Carmelita was having such a hard time getting their children to follow the rules of their home. It seemed to be harder since her husband Phil got this job that requires him to be on the road so much.

When Phil got home later that week, the two of them sat down and discussed how the children should have respect for their things and for their home. After all, the two of them worked hard to give them a home.

They decided to establish a reward system for the children. They would receive certain benefits and privileges for obeying the house rules.

"They also have got to understand that there are consequences for disobeying the house rules," said Phil.

"I know that's true," Carmelita responded. "But it's just so hard to stay on top of *everything* these days."

Phil acknowledged that he had been on the road too much to really help Carmelita. "Hopefully, after my first evaluation," he said, "I won't have to travel so much. That way, we can both work to make sure our system of reward and punishment is used to benefit our children."

AIM

After studying today's lesson, participants should understand that God has established the law for His people to live by, and He has promised a good life for those who obey Him.

SCRIPTURE TEXT

EXODUS 40:1 And the LORD spake unto Moses, saying,

2 On the first day of the first month shalt thou set up the tabernacle of the tent of the congregation.

3 And thou shalt put therein the ark of the testimony, and cover the ark with the veil.

4 And thou shalt bring in the table, and set in order the things that are to be set in order upon it; and thou shalt bring in the candlestick, and light the lamps thereof.

5 And thou shalt set the altar of gold for the incense before the ark of the testimony, and put the hanging of the door to the tabernacle.

6 And thou shalt set the altar of the burnt offering before the door of the tabernacle of the tent of the congregation.

7 And thou shalt set the laver between the tent of the congregation and the altar, and shalt put water therein.

8 And thou shalt set up the court round about, and hang up the hanging at the court gate.

9 And thou shalt take the anointing oil, and anoint the tabernacle, and all that is therein, and shalt hallow it, and all the vessels thereof: and it shall be holy.

LEVITICUS 26:2 Ye shall keep my sabbaths, and reverence my sanctuary: I am the LORD.

3 If ye walk in my statutes, and keep my commandments, and do them;

4 Then I will give you rain in due season, and the land shall yield her increase, and the trees of the field shall yield their fruit.

5 And your threshing shall reach unto the vintage, and the vintage shall reach unto the sowing time: and ye shall eat your bread to the full, and dwell in your land safely.

6 And I will give peace in the land, and ye shall lie down, and none shall make you afraid: and I will rid evil beasts out of the land, neither shall the sword go through your land.

11 And I will set my tabernacle among you: and my soul shall not abhor you.

12 And I will walk among you, and will be your God, and ye shall be my people.

13 I am the LORD your God, which brought you forth out of the land of Egypt, that ye should not be their bondmen; and I have broken the bands of your yoke, and made you go upright.

BIBLE BACKGROUND

God had begun the process of directing Israel in the proper way of life and worship. Once the tabernacle (or tent of meeting) was built, everything in it had to be consecrated. God gave Moses clear specifications concerning how the tabernacle was to be erected.

God's people also were to be dedicated for a purpose. Israel was to be a kingdom of priests and a holy nation (Exodus 19:6). Israel is to be holy in all things. Chapters 18-26 of Leviticus contain laws concerning right and holy conduct. Thus, this portion of Leviticus is known as the Holiness Code. It is a table of laws for those who were in covenant with God.

Unfortunately, Israel eventually began a cycle of rebellion and disobedience, which resulted in punishment by God. When their suffering became more than they felt they could withstand, they pleaded for God's mercy and returned to worshiping Him and obeying His laws. When they were once again comfortable with His blessings, Israel would fall back into a pattern of sinful behavior.

POINTS TO PONDER

1. *When did God command Moses to set up the tabernacle of the tent of meeting? (Exodus 40:2)*

   ____

   ____

   ____

2. *What was the first thing God told Moses to place inside the tabernacle? (v. 3)*

   ____

   ____

   ____

3. *Name at least three other items that God told Moses to put inside the tabernacle. (vv. 4-7)*

____

____

____

4. *What item was Moses to place at the entrance of the courtyard? (v. 8)*

____

____

____

5. *What was Moses to do with the anointing oil? (v. 9)*

____

____

____

6. *What did God command the people to do regarding the Sabbath and the sanctuary? (Leviticus 26:2)*

____

____

____

7. *What was the first promise God made to Israel in exchange for their obedience? (v. 3)*

____

____

____

8. *What kind of harvest did God promise the chosen people, if they were obedient? (v. 5)*

____

____

____

9. *What promise did God make to Israel concerning the land? (v. 6)*

 ____

 ____

 ____

10. *What did God promise concerning divine presence among the people? (vv. 11-13)*

 ____

 ____

 ____

LESSON AT-A-GLANCE

1. *Consecration of the Tabernacle (Exodus 40:1-9)*
2. *Rewards for Obedience (Leviticus 26:2-6, 11-13)*

EXPLORING THE MEANING

1. Consecration of the Tabernacle (Exodus 40:1-9)

God's requirement was that the tabernacle, all its contents, and Aaron and his sons be ceremonially consecrated and declared holy in service to the Lord. Nothing profane could be used in worshiping God. Moses was to anoint everything; thereby, symbolizing that they were set apart for the service of the Lord. It was important that everything in the tabernacle be consecrated, because it was more than a place of worship. The "tent of meeting" was the place to meet God. God was present at that place. God cannot be associated with anything that is unholy. God's command was that the tabernacle be set up on the first day of the year. This was about one year after the Exodus and about eight and one-half months after their arrival at Sinai. God chose a special time to institute His special place of worship and to consecrate the people and objects that were a part of that worship. This was not an insignificant matter. God commanded where every piece of furniture should be placed.

Two words figure prominently in God's instructions on erecting the Tabernacle: *hallow* and *anoint*. Each word occurs eight times in various forms. The major emphasis here is not the building itself, but on its purpose.

2. Rewards for Obedience (Leviticus 26:2-6; 11-13)

Leviticus 26 follows a pattern which is common to treaties in the ancient Near East; it provides blessings for those remaining loyal to God and curses for rejecting Him. This chapter is built upon the idea that human beings have the capacity to affect their own fate through their obedience or disobedience to God.

The conclusion to the Holiness Code (Leviticus 18-26) is a final appeal on the part of Yahweh. He outlines the rewards which will result from Israel's obedience to His law, as well as the punishment which will result from disobedience. It is likely that during Israel's religious festivals, the laws of the covenant between God and the nation were publicly proclaimed in an act of worship.

Because God's laws were themselves considered a part of God's blessing, the section which addresses reward is shorter than the section which addresses punishment. God wants the best life for the people. Divine covenant regulations established a way of life which promised providence, security, and peace. The essential blessings are that God's presence will remain with His people and that the promises of the covenant with Abraham will be fulfilled.

The list of rewards for obedience concentrates on two primary aspects of life. One reward is the fertility of the fields and the abundance of its crops. A fruitful harvest was essential to life, longevity, and stability. If they could not produce enough food to eat, Israel would be dependent upon other nations for food. What a sad commentary that would have been upon God's people!

God controls all of nature. The promise was not mainly for a sufficient and abundant crop. They would not be able to finish this year's crop before it was time to harvest the next year's. The key to abundant crops was simple—obey God's laws. Because they were God's people, God would take care of them and bless them. But how could they claim to be God's people if they would not obey? God's people obey God's commands!

The second reward is deliverance in times of war. Here, war is addressed in terms of the maintenance of national peace and security, rather than military aggression or expansion. God was going to establish His people in a land flowing with milk and honey. Such a land would be a desirous place to dwell. No doubt, other nations would look upon Israel and try to figure out ways to take what God had given them.

As God promised, throughout Israel's history, as long as they were obedient to Yahweh and did not serve other gods, they enjoyed peace as a nation. When they allowed themselves to be influenced by the gods of their neighbors, Israel nearly always faced military aggression.

It was to Israel's advantage to obey God. From the outset, Israel was not a nation of warriors. Israel did not have an aggressive spirit. They did not thrive on war or conflict. In fact, they often tended to be rather cowardly. The Hebrews attacked Moses because they faced uncertainty at the Red Sea. They were reticent to enter Canaan because the land was already inhabited. They needed God's protection in order to preserve peace; yet because of their disobedience, they would often find themselves vulnerable to attack.

God's challenge was issued to a nation, not to individuals. Therefore, it was up to the nation of Israel to remain loyal to God. No few groups of priests or faithful followers could keep God's law and expect that to satisfy the Lord. God wanted this for all people. The covenant was made with a *nation*. God's promises of both blessings and curses likewise were made to a nation.

DISCERNING MY DUTY

1. *Do God's promises concerning blessings for obedience still hold true today? Does God automatically punish people when they disobey His laws today?*
2. *When persons who have been obedient and faithful to the Lord experience trouble, such as hunger or tribulation, how can they deal with their troubles in light of God's promises?*
3. *When we suffer the consequences of disobeying God's laws, do we suffer because God is punishing us or because our suffering is simply a natural consequence of our disobedience?*

DECIDING MY RESPONSE

God's laws made sense for living. They were not simply a group of rules that God established to keep people in submission. The laws of the Holiness Code were partly for the people's own health and safety. The Code also helped people to maintain proper reverence in their relationship with God and with those He has called out for service.

The laws of God are not an outmoded code of conduct. God's laws are directives for healthy living and relating to one another. Many of the laws may seem irrelevant to our time. Perhaps, advances in medicine and technology have eliminated the need for certain restrictions. The fact remains that God's law is designed to maintain people in health and prosperity in every age.

Read through Leviticus chapters 18-26. List at least 10 laws which have helped to guide your life. Describe how adherence to those laws blessed and enhanced your life. Then list 10 laws which are largely not observed today. How has disobedience to those laws hindered or crippled our society in some way? (You may cite specific laws or general categories of God's law.)

LIGHT ON THE HEAVY

TENT OF MEETING. Also known as the tabernacle, it was a sacred tent which served as a portable and provisional sanctuary where God met His people. Tents were dwelling places for nomads.

The original tent of meeting was a provisional structure where God met with the Children of Israel. It is believed that, at first, only Moses actually entered the tent to meet with God. Joshua protected and cared for the tent. After the Hebrews made the golden calf, God refused to acknowledge them as His people and would no longer dwell in their midst. Because there was now distance between God and the people, Moses moved the tent of meeting outside the camp. Ultimately, God promised to once again do great things in the midst of Israel (Exodus 34:16).

Moses called it "the tent of meeting" because it was the place of revelation. God met His people there when the pillar of cloud descended to the doorway of the tent (Exodus 34:9).

Based on information from *Holman Bible Dictionary*, Trent Butler, general editor. Nashville: Broadman & Holman Publishers, 1991, p. 1316-1317.

ARK OF THE TESTIMONY. Also known as the Ark of the Covenant. The ark is the container for the Ten Commandments and the key symbol of God's presence with the people of Israel.

The ark of ancient Israel has many names, all of which convey the holy sense of God's presence. The Hebrew word for ark means "box" or "coffin." The word *covenant* in the name, Ark of the Covenant, defines the ark based on its original purpose, which was a container for the stone tablets on which the Ten Commandments were written. The ark dates back to Moses at Mount Sinai, but its origin is mysterious. There are contrasting accounts of how the ark was made in the Pentateuch (the first five books of the Bible). After the people sinned by worshiping the golden calf and the original Decalogue tablets were broken, Moses made a plain box of acacia wood as a container to receive the new tables of the Law.

The ark is also known by several names, including "the ark of God," the more elaborate name, "the ark of the Lord," and "the ark of the covenant of the Lord of hosts (Yahweh Sabaoth) who is enthroned on the cherubim."

Based on information from *Holman Bible Dictionary*, pp. 98-99.

Accept God's Guidance

Based on Numbers 13:25-31; 14:6-10, 28-30

DEFINING THE ISSUE

Remember the old TV program called "Mission Impossible"? A contact person would receive instructions regarding a very difficult assignment from the government, such as rescuing a prisoner of war from behind enemy lines. After the assignment was received, the cassette tape would self-destruct. The instructions always included the phrase, "If you decide to accept this mission and get caught, we will disavow any knowledge of your actions. Good luck!" The contact person would then sit down, go through a file, and select photographs of individuals who had a certain area of expertise to comprise a team that could get the job done. The individuals were contacted and would accept the challenge.

In our lesson, Moses received an assignment with no proof of its source other than God's word. He selected his team to begin the first stages of the mission. In observing how the Israelites responded to their assignment, perhaps we will see ourselves and gain insight in our responses to assignments we receive from God that seemingly fit the title of a "mission impossible."

AIM

By the end of the lesson, participants will be able to retell the story of the 12 spies, their reports, and the Israelites' reaction.

Participants will understand the willingness of the Lord to guide their lives and commit themselves to seeking, finding, and doing God's will.

SCRIPTURE TEXT

NUMBERS 13:25 And they returned from searching of the land after forty days.

26 And they went and came to Moses, and to Aaron, and to all the congregation of the children of Israel, unto the wilderness of Paran, to Kadesh; and brought back word unto them, and unto all the congregation, and shewed them the fruit of the land.

27 And they told him, and said, We came unto the land whither thou sentest us, and surely it floweth with milk and honey; and this is the fruit of it.

28 Nevertheless the people be strong that dwell in the land, and the cities are walled, and very great: and moreover we saw the children of Anak there.

29 The Amalekites dwell in the land of the south: and the Hittites, and the Jebusites, and the Amorites, dwell in the mountains: and the Canaanites dwell by the sea, and by the coast of Jordan.

30 And Caleb stilled the people before Moses, and said, Let us go up at once, and possess it; for we are well able to overcome it.

31 But the men that went up with him said, We be not able to go up against the people; for they are stronger than we.

14:6 And Joshua the Son of Nun, and Caleb the son of Jephunneh, which were of them that searched the land, rent their clothes:

7 And they spake unto all the company of the children of Israel, saying, The land, which we passed through to search it, is an exceeding good land.

8 If the Lord delight in us, then he will bring us into this land, and give it us; a land which floweth with milk and honey.

9 Only rebel not ye against the Lord, neither fear ye the people of the land; for they are bread for us: their defence is departed from them, and the Lord is with us: fear them not.

10 But all the congregation bade stone them with stones. And the glory of the Lord appeared in the tabernacle of the congregation before all the children of Israel.

14:28 Say unto them, As truly as I live, saith the Lord, as ye have spoken in mine ears, so will I do to you:

29 Your carcases shall fall in this wilderness; and all that were numbered of you, according to your whole number, from twenty years old and upward, which have murmured against me.

30 Doubtless ye shall not come into the land, concerning which I sware to make you dwell therein, save Caleb the son of Jephunneh, and Joshua the son of Nun.

BIBLE BACKGROUND

The Book of Numbers is the fourth book of the Torah (Hebrew for the "books of law"). It covers a period of approximately 40 years in the Israelites' quest to acquire the Promised Land of Canaan. The name of the book is reflective of the census Moses took of the people. In the verses of chapter 13, prior to where our lesson begins, we find God instructing Moses to send one man from each of the 12 tribes of Israel to spy out the land of Canaan. In verses 18-20, Moses gives them specific instructions about the type of information they are to obtain. Our lesson begins with the report of their findings.

POINTS TO PONDER

1. *What did the people, who spied out the Promised Land, find that was good? (Numbers 13:23, 27)*

 ____

 ____

 ____

 ____

2. *What did they find that scared them? (v. 28)*

 ____

 ____

 ____

 ____

3. *Why did the people not want to go to possess the land? (v. 31)*

 ____

 ____

 ____

 ____

4. *What argument did Joshua and Caleb give to address the people's fears? (14:9)*

   ____

   ____

   ____

5. *What was God's response to the Israelites' disobedience? (v. 29)*

   ____

   ____

   ____

6. *What was God's response to the obedience of Joshua and Caleb? (v. 30)*

   ____

   ____

   ____

LESSON AT-A-GLANCE

1. *The spies report on the land (Numbers 13:25-28)*
2. *Their suggested plan of action (vv. 30-31)*
3. *Joshua and Caleb's words of encouragement (Numbers 14:6-10)*
4. *God's response (vv. 28-30)*

EXPLORING THE MEANING

1. The spies report on the land (Numbers 13:25-28)

The number 40 is often used in the Bible to represent a time of testing and strengthening. It is significant as a symbolic and sacred number. Forty years is the approximate length of a generation. Forty days or years was the usual length of time for critical situations of punishment, fasting, repentance, and vigil. (*The Interpreter's Dictionary of the Bible*, Abingdon Press, Nashville: 1984, p. 565). It took the spies 40 days to evaluate the land and its people. This must have been a testing time for the 12 men who went on the expedition.

Their report gives us a clue as to how well they did at this time of testing. They informed Moses, Aaron, and the congregation of Israelites that there was good news and bad news. The good news was that the produce of the land was fantastic. The phrase "floweth with milk and honey" implies that the land contained all of the essentials necessary for producing nutritious abundant harvests and healthy animals. As Moses had instructed, they brought samples of the produce in the form of pomegranates, figs, and grapes (Numbers 13:26-27).

The bad news was that the cities were huge and protected with walls, and the people were giants, "children of Anak" (13:33).

2. Their suggested plan of action (vv. 30-31)

The people became upset with the report of the fortified cities and their strong inhabitants. Caleb calmed the people down and told them to take immediate action. He probably sensed that if they thought about it too long they wouldn't go. He also expressed his confidence that they would be able to take the land with no problem. The other men who had gone with him, except Joshua, disagreed and stated that they would not be able to defeat these giant people because they were stronger than the Hebrews.

There are people today whom we would call pessimistic because they have a defeatist attitude about all challenging situations. They focus on the negatives and give up without considering options that could enable them to address difficult situations. They forget that God is able to help us face all challenges.

The verses between 13:31 and 14:6 tell us that the group often had a strong following and gave an "evil" report (13:32-33). Unfortunately, the people tapped into their fear and became hysterical, talking against Moses, Aaron, and God and began to form a "Back to Egypt" committee.

3. Joshua and Caleb's words of encouragement (Numbers 14:6-10)

The formula "son of," which is used in verse six and in the listing in Numbers 13:4-15 of all those chosen from the 12 tribes to scout out the land, is a phrase used to emphasize ancestry. It means "descendant of" and could also indicate a people's political, civic, geographical, and cultural affiliation (*The Black Presence in the Bible*, Chicago: Black Light Fellowship, 1991, p. 37). Joshua was from the tribe of Ephraim and Caleb from the tribe of Judah.

Joshua and Caleb's gesture of "renting" or tearing their clothes was a usual expression of grief to show the people how serious they felt about taking the land. They again emphasized how good the land was and how God would give the Israelites that abundant land, if they pleased Him by being obedient. They pointed the people in the direction of the wrath of God, which should have concerned the people much more than fortified cities with strong occupants (14:9). With God on their side, the Israelites did not have to fear their enemies, who were like "bread" to them, when compared with God's power. Unfortunately, the people's fear caused them to forget what God had already done. They were so adamant about not challenging the people who occupied the land that they wanted to kill those who tried to talk them into doing it. They refused to accept the mission.

But before we criticize the Israelites, a little self-analysis might be helpful. Do we receive "tapes" (like the man in "Mission

Impossible") from God with challenging situations that also contain abundant blessings? Do these "tapes" self-destruct after we hear them, and our fear keeps us from accepting the mission?

4. God's response (vv. 28-30)

In Numbers 14:11-27, we find that God is fed up with the Israelites' lack of faith, in spite of all that He has done for them. He tells Moses that He will kill them with some sort of disease, and they will no longer be His chosen people. From Moses He will make a greater nation of people. Moses intercedes with God, imploring Him not to do this. Moses points out that the Egyptians will tell the people of Canaan about the God of the Israelites and how they were all killed. Furthermore, the people of Canaan will say that since God was not able to bring the Israelites into the land of Canaan, He killed them off in the wilderness. Moses proceeds to praise God for His patience, mercy, and forgiving nature toward the Children of Israel.

God is merciful and just, and He agrees not to destroy the people as a nation, but tells Moses that the present generation will suffer the consequences. Verse two of Numbers 14 tells us of the people murmuring against their leaders and God. To "murmur" is to mumble under one's breath, usually so the subject of the murmuring can hear the voice, but not the words. God tells Moses to inform the people that there is not a whisper or mumble that He can't hear, and that everyone 20 years old and over will not enter the Promised Land but will die while wandering in the wilderness. The exceptions were Caleb and Joshua.

It is interesting to note that Moses was not on the list of exceptions. He was not allowed to enter the Promised Land, but for another reason: his disobedience occurred later (Numbers 20:7-12).

God's mission for the Israelites only became impossible when they refused to accept it. It is good to remember the examples of Joshua and Caleb when faced with our personal missions. Faith makes "impossible" missions possible.

DISCERNING MY DUTY

1. *If God had already promised the land to the Israelites, why did He instruct them to send out a scouting party?*
2. *Were the men who opposed Caleb and Joshua being practical and realistic? Why or why not?*
3. *How did the "evil report" given by those who did not want to possess the land differ from the original report and why?*
4. *God seemed to be particularly upset with the people murmuring against Him. Why?*
5. *What was it about Caleb and Joshua that caused God to exclude them from His judgment?*

DECIDING MY RESPONSE

Often in our society, issues arise in which the majority of the people will support the side contrary to God's law and His will for us. What does this lesson say to us regarding how we should react when faced by a majority or a minority on issues such as gun control, abortion, homosexuality, capital punishment, or promiscuity?

Identify a mission you believe God has given to you, but that you have difficulty in accepting. Begin evaluating why you are reluctant to accept it. Look at the positives and negatives involved. Focus on the positives and how you and God can address the negatives. Then take steps necessary to get started. If you have not yet identified how God wants to use you, begin asking Him to reveal His will to you.

LIGHT ON THE HEAVY

JOSHUA. Joshua was called by his family name Hosea which means "salvation." At the Exodus, Joshua was a young man. Moses chose him as a personal assistant. In the plains by the Jordan, he was formally consecrated as Moses's successor to the military leadership, to work in coordination with Eleazar the Priest. He was then probably about 70 years old. Joshua occupied and consolidated the area of Gilgal, fought successful campaigns against Canaanite confederacies, and directed further operations as long as the united efforts of Israel were required. Joshua died at the age of 110. (*The New Bible Dictionary*, Wheaton: IL, Tyndale House, 1984, p. 621)

Love the Lord Your God

Based on Deuteronomy 6:1-13

DEFINING THE ISSUE

Fourteen-year-old Tamika simply couldn't understand why her parents were so strict. It was summer vacation and all the other kids on her block were allowed to stay out long after dark. But, she had to be in the house by sundown.

Tamika felt that if her parents really loved her as much as they claimed, they wouldn't be so cruel. They would allow her to enjoy her life and stop making all these silly rules.

One day, several of Tamika's friends made plans to go to a drive-in movie in their 16-year-old friend's car. The last show didn't end until after midnight. Tamika knew that she would never be allowed to stay out that late. Her best friend Charmaine's parents were a lot more lenient. The two of them hatched a plan for Tamika to spend the night at Charmaine's house. They would go to the drive-in and Tamika's parents would never know the difference.

The plan worked to perfection. Tamika was allowed to stay the night, and they all went to the drive-in. On the way home, on a dark deserted street, the car had a flat tire. None of the girls knew how to change a tire.

A car pulled up beside them and a man with a smiling face asked, "Do you girls need some help?"

One of the girls called out, "We've got a flat tire. Can you help us change it?"

"Sure," came the reply, "I'll help." But, as the man got out of the car, he pulled out the biggest gun Tamika had ever seen. He took all of their purses and ordered them to lie face down in the street while he searched them.

As Tamika lay on the ground, she prayed, and promised God that if she got out of this alive, she would never disobey her parents again. After searching their car, the man jumped into his own car and laughingly drove away. Tamika lay on the ground, too frightened to move. She realized now that the rules of her parents were given out of love and concern for her well-being.

The focus of this lesson is on the laws God gave to the nation of Israel through His Prophet Moses. As a loving Father, God does not arbitrarily issue edicts designed to deprive us of pleasure. He gives us these laws because He loves us and knows what's best for us. He wants us to prosper in body, mind, and spirit.

AIM

By the end of the lesson, participants will be able to understand how God demonstrates His love for us and explain how we demonstrate our love back to Him and commit ourselves to faithfully study His Word and live accordingly.

SCRIPTURE TEXT

DEUTERONOMY 6:1 Now these are the commandments, the statutes, and the judgments, which the Lord your God commanded to teach you, that ye might do them in the land whither ye go to possess it:

2 That thou mightest fear the Lord thy God, to keep all his statutes and his commandments, which I command thee, thou, and thy son, and thy son's son, all the days of thy life; and that thy days may be prolonged.

3 Hear therefore, O Israel, and observe to do it; that it may be well with thee, and that ye may increase mightily, as the Lord God of thy fathers hath promised thee, in the land that floweth with milk and honey.

4 Hear, O Israel: The Lord our God is one Lord:

5 And thou shalt love the Lord thy God with all thine heart, and with all thy soul, and with all thy might.

6 And these words, which I command thee this day, shall be in thine heart:

7 And thou shalt teach them diligently unto thy children, and shalt talk of them when thou sittest in thine house, and when thou walkest by the way, and when thou liest down, and when thou risest up.

8 And thou shalt bind them for a sign upon thine hand, and they shall be as frontlets between thine eyes.

9 And thou shalt write them upon the posts of thy house, and on thy gates.

10 And it shall be, when the Lord thy God shall have brought thee into the land which he sware unto thy fathers, to Abraham, to Isaac, and to Jacob, to give thee great and goodly cities, which thou buildedst not,

> 11 And houses full of all good things, which thou filledst not, and wells digged, which thou diggedst not, vineyards and olive trees, which thou plantedst not; when thou shalt have eaten and be full;
>
> 12 Then beware lest thou forget the Lord, which brought thee forth out of the land of Egypt, from the house of bondage.
>
> 13 Thou shalt fear the Lord thy God, and serve him, and shalt swear by his name.

BIBLE BACKGROUND

The Book of Deuteronomy records the renewal of God's covenant with Israel. The original mixed multitude that left Egypt wandered in the desert for 40 years and died. Now, on the east bank of the Jordan River, Moses leads the people in renewing the covenant.

In the first four chapters, Moses recounts how God demonstrated His love and care for Israel by delivering them out of Egypt. He reminds them of how the people responded to that love with disobedience and faithlessness. In chapters five through 26, Moses points out that the basis for their relationship with God is love. This love relationship was to be demonstrated by their obeying God's laws. In chapters 27-30, the original covenant is ratified anew and the conditions are explained to this new generation of people. Chapters 31-34 are the transition chapters. A new leader is appointed, and a wandering people are about to become a settled nation.

The Book of Deuteronomy provides Christians with a threefold truth about God: 1) Because of what He has done in the past, we should trust Him with our future; 2) Because He has chosen us, we should obey Him completely; 3) Because of Who He is, we should love Him above all else.

POINTS TO PONDER

1. *The Israelites were about to enter a land filled with people who believed in many gods. What was the primary concept the Israelites were to remember and teach their families? (v. 12)*

 ____

 ____

 ____

2. *Phylacteries (fy-LACK-tu-rees) and mezuzahs (me-ZU-zahs) are symbols used to remind the Israelites of their relationship with God. How were these symbols to be displayed? (vv. 9-10)*

 ____

 ____

 ____

3. *The Israelites had endured 40 years of harsh desert life. They were about to settle down in a land filled with abundant crops and water wells. The wells had been dug by other nations. To what great danger did Moses alert them?*

 ____

 ____

 ____

LESSON AT-A-GLANCE

1. *Purpose of obedience (Deuteronomy 6:1-5)*
2. *Practice of obedience (vv. 6-9)*
3. *Peril to disobedience (vv. 10-13)*

EXPLORING THE MEANING

1. Purpose of obedience (Deuteronomy 6:1-5)

The Israelites are encamped on the plains of Moab, on the eastern edge of the Jordan valley. They are poised to enter "the land of milk and honey," which God had promised to their parents 40 years ago. As the mediator between God and the people, Moses is concerned that they and all their future generations maintain the proper reverence for God and His Law. He, therefore, reviewed the covenant with them.

After reviewing the Ten Commandments (chapter 5), Moses began his discourse by reminding the people that these are not his laws, but the commands of God Himself (6:1). When we sin, we always sin against God even though we may not always commit an offense against society.

Moses tells the people in verse three that if they will both hear and obey God's law, all will go well for them, and they will prosper in this new and fertile land. Blessings are the result of acknowledging God and continually obeying His word. We are not blessed by just hearing great teachings or fiery sermons, but by putting the messages of these teachings and sermons into daily practice.

2. Practice of obedience (vv. 6-9)

The greatest reason for obeying God is love, not blessings. Moses continues his teachings by affirming that God is one. Because of His love for His creation, God has chosen to reveal Himself to His creation. He has revealed Himself to us as One person (Deuteronomy 6:4). He is totally unique and set apart from all creation. He is the one absolute ruler, with one absolute law and absolute power. The very order of creation is a result of God's oneness.

God's revelation of Himself to us demands a response from us. The only fitting response to God's divine revelation of love is to love Him back with every fiber of our being (v. 5). This means our whole-hearted, unreserved, and total commitment to God.

Moses encourages the Israelites to teach God's laws in their homes and to children (v. 7). They are to teach them diligently both with formal times of family Scripture study, and informally during normal conversation. The word of God should be clearly seen in our households, by what we teach and by our lives. Our family should know us by our words and our actions.

The Israelites are instructed to wear certain symbols and attach other symbols to their homes (vv. 8-9) These symbols were signs of their dedication to God and constant reminders to them of His Law. Jewish men often wore small containers on their foreheads and upper left arms called phylacteries. These containers were portions of Old Testament scripture. Similar containers called *mezuzahs* were attached to the door frames of their homes. For Christians today, the Holy Spirit brings God's Word to our remembrance (John 14:26), but many people have found value in having visible reminders of God's Word in our homes.

3. Peril to disobedience (vv. 10-13)

Often the greatest threat to our loving relationship with God is not temptation or trial, but times of peace and well-being. Moses warned the Israelites not to forget God when they entered the new land with all its abundance.

DISCERNING MY DUTY

1. *How does the revelation of God's oneness refute the claims of the atheists, cultists, and pagans?*

2. *What is the basis of our relationship with God? How is this demonstrated horizontally and vertically?*
3. *Why do periods of peace and prosperity tend to make people forget about their relationship with God?*
4. *Many people in our society believe that they are too evil or too bad to have a relationship with God. They feel that they must somehow get themselves ready before they come to God. How can we believers share with these people that our relationship with God is based on love and not merit?*

DECIDING MY RESPONSE

Believers are often obedient to God because they want blessings from God or recognition from people. Our primary motivation for obedience should be love. This week, evaluate your motivations for being obedient to God. Petition God to help you grow to the point where your actions are motivated solely by love.

LIGHT ON THE HEAVY

MEZUZAH. When the angel of death passed over Egypt, killing all firstborn males, Jewish families were protected by the blood of the paschal lamb on the doorposts of their homes (Exodus 12:23). Today many Jews attach a *mezuzah* to their doorposts as a reminder of God's presence and the Jewish people's redemption from Egypt.

The mezuzah (Hebrew, meaning "doorpost") is a small case containing a parchment on which the following prayer is written: "Hear, O Israel: the Lord our God is Lord: And thou shalt love the Lord thy God with all thy heart, and with all thy soul, and with all thy might. And these words which I command thee this day, shall be in thine heart: And thou shalt teach them diligently unto thy children, and shalt talk of them when thou sittest in thine house, and when thou walkest by the way, when thou liest down, and when thou risest up. And thou shalt bind them for a sign upon thine hand, and they shall be as frontlets between thine eyes. And thou shalt write them upon the posts of thy house, and on thy gates" (Deuteronomy 6:4-9).

The mezuzah is a Jewish family's daily reminder of their responsibility to God and their community. It is a sign to the community that this home is one where the laws of God reign supreme. (J. I. Packer, et. al, *The Bible Almanac*, p. 387)

None Like Moses

Based on Deuteronomy 34:1-12

DEFINING THE ISSUE

Harriet Tubman, the "Black Moses," lived, and then she died. The Reverend Dr. Martin Luther King, Jr. lived, and then he died. Chicago Mayor Harold Washington lived, and then he died.

All were great Black leaders. All served their generation well and led Black people in making tremendous strides toward freedom and justice. Despite their greatness, leaders die just like the people they lead.

A leader's greatness is measured partly in the kind of heritage which he/she leaves. Moses was a great leader. He left a great heritage. One definition of "heritage" is "something other than property passed down from preceding generations, legacy, tradition." Have you ever asked yourself, "What kind of heritage will I leave for the next generation after I am gone?" If you have never asked yourself that question, why don't you pause and ask it now?

AIM

To help students recall certain positive attributes which characterized Moses' life, feel the need to emulate these traits, and commit themselves to acquire these traits, so they can be left as a legacy for those who follow.

SCRIPTURE TEXT

> DEUTERONOMY 34:1 And Moses went up from the plains of Moab unto the mountain of Nebo, to the top of Pisgah, that is over against Jericho. And the LORD showed him all the land of Gilead, unto Dan,
>
> 2 And all Naphtali, and the land of Ephraim, and Manasseh, and all the land of Judah, unto the utmost sea,
>
> 3 And the south, and the plain of the valley of Jericho, the city of palm trees, unto Zoar.
>
> 4 And the LORD said unto him, This is the land which I sware unto Abraham, unto Isaac, and unto Jacob, saying, I will give it unto thy seed: I have caused thee to see it with thine eyes, but thou shalt not go over thither.
>
> 5 So Moses the servant of the LORD died there in the land of Moab, according to the word of the LORD.
>
> 6 And he buried him in a valley in the land of Moab, over against Bethpeor: but no man knoweth of his sepulcher unto this day.
>
> 7 And Moses was an hundred and twenty years old when he died: His eye was not dim, nor his natural force abated.
>
> 8 And the children of Israel wept for Moses in the plains of Moab thirty days: so the days of weeping and mourning for Moses were ended.

9 And Joshua the son of Nun was full of the spirit of wisdom; for Moses had laid his hands upon him: and the children of Israel hearkened unto him, and did as the LORD commanded Moses.

10 And there arose not a prophet since in Israel like unto Moses, whom the LORD knew face to face,

11 In all the signs and the wonders, which the LORD sent him to do in the land of Egypt to Pharaoh, and to all his servants, and to all his land,

12 And in all that mighty hand, and in all the great terror which Moses showed in the sight of all Israel.

BIBLE BACKGROUND

Moses was a great deliverer of God. God used him in outstanding ways during his 120-year life. He was a powerful leader and emancipator. He led the Children of Israel from Egyptian bondage, through 40 years of wilderness wanderings, right up to the brink of the land promised to them by God.

But then, as happens to all leaders, the time came for Moses to die. In a most gracious gesture, God called His servant Moses to the top of Mount Nebo to view the land promised to Abraham, Isaac, and Jacob.

After viewing the land, Moses died there on the mountain, and God Himself gave His great servant a private burial. The people mourned the death of their leader. What did Moses leave behind? What was his heritage?

For one thing, Moses left behind a gifted and Spirit-filled leader named Joshua. Even though Moses died, the work of liberation and nation-building continued through Joshua.

Second, Moses left behind a living and glowing testimony. He had served with excellence as a prophet of God who, like none other, knew God "face to face." The reputation of Moses spread far and near because of the miracles performed by him in Egypt and for the Children of Israel. The life and formidable presence of Moses left an indelible print in the sands of time.

This final chapter of Deuteronomy (34:1-12) is a "brief prose narrative which forms an easy sequel to 32:48-52." (*Deuteronomy*; J.A. Thompson; IVP; p. 318)

Prior to his death, Moses commissioned Joshua as God's new leader of Israel (Deuteronomy 31:1-8). Also, God instructed Moses to write a song and speak its words to the Children of Israel (31:19, 21, 22, 30ff.). God said that this song would "be a witness for me against the children of Israel" (Deuteronomy 31:19). In the midst of their rebellion, this song would remind the Children of Israel of their covenant relationship to the Lord.

On the same day Moses finished speaking his song to the nation, the Lord called him to view the Promised Land and to die on the mountain (Deuteronomy 32:48ff.). Deuteronomy 33:1-29 records Moses' final blessing upon the Children of Israel, tribe by tribe.

The last days of Moses can also be studied in the following texts: Numbers 27:12-14; Deuteronomy 3:23-28, 32:48-52.

POINTS TO PONDER

1. *From what mountain did Moses view the Promised Land? (Deuteronomy 34:1)*

   ____

   ____

   ____

2. *What did God prohibit Moses from doing even though God allowed him to view the Promised Land? (34:4)*

3. *Where did Moses die? (34:5)*

4. *How old was Moses when he died, and what was the state of his physical health? (34:7)*

5. *For what period of time did the Children of Israel mourn Moses' death? (34:8)*

6. *Who became Moses' successor? (34:9)*

7. *How is Moses described? (34:5, 10)*

LESSON AT-A-GLANCE

1. *Moses' view of the Promised Land (Deuteronomy 34:1-4)*
2. *Moses' death (vv. 5-8)*
3. *Moses' heritage (vv. 9-12)*

EXPLORING THE MEANING

1. Moses' view of the Promised Land (Deuteronomy 34:1-4)

The new generation of Israelites had been fully instructed by Moses. The Commandments of God which had been originally given to Moses were rewritten by Moses, reviewed, and committed to the Levites and deposited beside the ark of the covenant (31:9ff., 24ff.). The people were now waiting in the plains of Moab (32:49), on the brink of entering the Land of Promise.

Moses was 120 years old. He was not able to lead the Children of Israel as he had led them through the wilderness over the past nearly 40 years (Deuteronomy 31:1-2). God had prohibited Moses from entering the Promised Land because of his transgression at Meribah (Deuteronomy 32:51-52; 3:23-27; Numbers 27:12-14; cf. Numbers 20:1-13). It was now time to die.

What a gracious gesture of God to permit His servant Moses to view the Promised Land. Moses had experienced unusual intimacy with God. Indeed, he knew the Lord "face to face." He had been mightily used by God to lead a people from slavery to freedom. Despite his faltering at Meribah, God affirms the approval of His servant by allowing him to have a panoramic view of the Canaan Land.

The place of viewing was the mountain of "Nebo" (Deuteronomy 34:1) on the peak of "Pisgah." The word "Pisgah" denotes "any jagged ridge, and would describe aptly the mountain's highest peak, Jebel Osha, as seen from beneath." (*New Bible Commentary*; Eerdmans; R.K. Harrison). "Abarim" is a word used in 32:49, and is the plural of the word meaning "across" or "beyond," referring to the mountainous range in northwest Moab, overlooking the north end of the Dead Sea. Cf. Numbers 21:11; 27:12

This last act of Moses was an act of obedience to his Lord. He wanted Moses to see the land which He swore to give to Abraham, Isaac, and Jacob. (Deuteronomy 32:49; 34:4; Exodus 33:1) Perhaps, Moses' view of the land "had some legal significance. There is some evidence that this was part of a legal process. A man 'viewed' what he was to possess." (*Deuteronomy;* Thompson)

2. Moses' death (vv. 5-8)

Having viewed the Promised Land, "the servant of the Lord died there in the land of Moab" just as the Lord had said Moses would. (v. 5; cf. 32:50) The phrase, "he buried him" most naturally refers to God. This is confirmed by the statement made by the recorder that "no man knoweth of his sepulcher unto this day" (v. 6). "There was something special about the burial of Moses . . . man did not have a part in it" (*Deuteronomy*; P.C. Craigie; NICOT; p. 405). Evidently, Moses was buried in the same general area in which Israel had assembled to hear his final addresses. (Deuteronomy 3:29; 4:46) His body was hidden from humanity, though not from spiritual beings. (cf. Jude 9)

A statement is made (v. 7) about the physical well-being of Moses at the time of his death. Though according to 31:2 Moses was no longer able to fulfill all the burdensome responsibilities of leadership, neither his vision nor vigor were impaired. The reference to the "natural force" of Moses may be a reference to "a man's sexual force, either literally or as a means of describing full health" (*Deuteronomy*; Craigie).

The fact that Moses' age at the time of death was 120 years (cf. 31:2) may also carry symbolic meaning, besides highlighting his life of three generations of 40 years each. "In Ancient Egypt the epitaph 'he died aged one hundred and ten' was the highest accolade which could be bestowed upon an individual of outstanding character and practical ability . . . By these standards Moses had led an unusually rich, productive and beneficial life" (*NBC*; Harrison). Moses was mourned the same number of days as Aaron his brother. (Deuteronomy 34:8; Numbers 20:29)

3. Moses' heritage (vv. 9-12)

The leader Moses left a great heritage. One aspect of this heritage was the perpetuation of his nation-building work through his successor "Joshua the son of Nun" (v. 9).

When Moses set apart Joshua for the office of leadership, Moses laid his hands upon Joshua and invested Joshua with a portion of his authority. This was done according to the command of God (cf. Numbers 27:18-23). Since Joshua was already filled with the Spirit of God, Moses was only visibly affirming the gifts already given by God (Deuteronomy 34:9; cf. Numbers 27:18). The Israelites responded by obeying Joshua as their new leader (v. 9b).

Another aspect of Moses' heritage was his great testimony. Moses was a "servant" over God's house (v. 5; Hebrews 3:3-5). Moses was a one-of-a-kind "prophet" known for his intimate knowledge and fellowship with God (v. 10; Exodus 33:11). Surely Moses typifies Christ whom he prophesied would come as God's Prophet (Deuteronomy 18:15). Moses was a great miracle-worker, both in the areas of liberating acts from Egypt (v. 11) and preserving acts for the nation of Israel (v. 12).

Thus, Moses left a great heritage—in gifted leadership and in a living testimony. Those of us who would aspire to emulate the life of Moses would do well to remember the heritage he left for generations to come.

DISCERNING MY DUTY

1. *Moses was a great prophet of the Lord. Yet, Moses was not allowed to enter the Promised Land. Why not? What, if any, similar things happen to great servants of the Lord today?*
2. *What positive trait observed in the life of Moses would you like to emulate? Why?*

DECIDING MY RESPONSE

Many Christians know little about the details of Moses' life. During the week, make it your purpose to read an encyclopedia article on the life of Moses. Keep notes of information which appeal to you for further study.

LIGHT ON THE HEAVY

PROMISE LAND. Moses was shown the Promised Land by God from the top of Mt. Nebo (Deuteronomy 34:1). "The enumeration given in verses 1a-3 follows a large anti-clockwise circle from north to south Gilead, Dan, Naphtali, Ephraim, Manasseh, Judah as far as the Mediterranean Sea, the Negeb, and finally the Plain . . . or Valley of Jericho (the city of palm trees). (Judges 1:16; 3:12, 13)" (*Deuteronomy*; Thompson). "Jebel Osha on a clear day, agrees exactly with this description in every detail, from snow-capped Hermon, Galilee, the Mount of Olives, to Bethlehem, to the Dead Sea and beyond" (*New Bible Commentary*).

Principles of Faith

Based on Joshua 3:7-17

DEFINING THE ISSUE

Tameka Johnson had been involved in a terrible automobile accident. After many tests and spending several days in the hospital, the doctors concluded that she would never walk again. Tameka's legs were crushed beyond repair, but she sensed the voice of God telling her to be strong and to cast all of her cares upon Him. She believed God, and silently began to pray. She told the doctors that she was determined to walk once again.

For several months, Tameka received physical therapy and practiced walking. It was very difficult and sometimes she wanted to give up, but she kept sensing "the voice" telling her to get up and try again. She had a little faith in herself, but she believed in the power of God. Day by day, and little by little, Tameka regained strength in her legs and eventually was able to walk, jump, and jog, as she had done before.

Has God ever done anything "miraculous" for you? Acting on faith at times can seem silly and even impossible, can't it? But if God has spoken, even the impossible is possible by faith. Today, we explore the miraculous—the impossible, which is possible when we obey the voice of the Lord.

AIM

By the end of the lesson, participants will be able to retell correctly the story of Joshua and the crossing of the Jordan River, understand the "Seven Principles of Faith" discussed in the lesson, and will participate in an "act with faith" project with the class.

SCRIPTURE TEXT

> JOSHUA 3:7 And the Lord said unto Joshua, This day will I begin to magnify thee in the sight of all Israel, that they may know that, as I was with Moses, so I will be with thee.
>
> 8 And thou shalt command the priests that bear the ark of the covenant, saying, When ye are come to the brink of the water of Jordan, ye shall stand still in Jordan.
>
> 9 And Joshua said unto the children of Israel, Come hither, and hear the words of the Lord your God.
>
> 10 And Joshua said, Hereby ye shall know that the living God is among you, and that he will without fail drive out from before you the Canaanites, and the Hittites, and the Hivites, and the Perizzites, and the Girgashites, and the Amorites, and the Jebusites.
>
> 11 Behold, the ark of the covenant of the Lord of all the earth passeth over before you into Jordan.
>
> 12 Now therefore take you twelve men out of the tribes of Israel, out of every tribe a man.
>
> 13 And it shall come to pass, as soon as the soles of the feet of the priests that bear the ark of the Lord, the Lord

of all the earth, shall rest in the waters of Jordan, that the waters of Jordan shall be cut off from the waters that come down from above; and they shall stand upon an heap.

14 And it came to pass, when the people removed from their tents, to pass over Jordan, and the priests bearing the ark of the covenant before the people;

15 And as they that bare the ark were come unto Jordan, and the feet of the priests that bare the ark were dipped in the brim of the water, (for Jordan overfloweth all his banks all the time of harvest,)

16 That the waters which came down from above stood and rose up upon an heap very far from the city Adam, that is beside Zaretan: and those that came down toward the sea of the plain, even the salt sea, failed, and were cut off; and the people passed over right against Jericho.

17 And the priests that bare the ark of the covenant of the Lord stood firm on dry ground in the midst of Jordan, and all the Israelites passed over on dry ground, until all the people were passed clean over Jordan.

BIBLE BACKGROUND

In this study, we explore the story of Joshua preparing to enter the Promised Land of Canaan. "Joshua," chapter two, records his sending out spies to study the land areas, especially Jericho. Joshua is confident, because the report of Rahab indicates that the people of Canaan have heard about the God of Israel (Joshua 2:9).

In this study, we will examine the crossing of the Jordan by the Children of Israel. As we study this passage, we will also discover seven principles of faith.

Faith principle #1—Faith purifies and prepares our hearts and minds to receive from God. The believers will not come to God on their own terms but will first seek the Lord by consecrating their life to Him. For only then can they truly know God and hear from God. The mind must be ready to believe and receive, even if it cannot fully conceive.

Israel has consecrated itself and we will now follow this adventure as it unfolds in the lesson.

POINTS TO PONDER

1. *God made two promises to Joshua as he began to lead the Children of Israel. What are they? (Joshua 3:7)*

   ____

   ____

   ____

2. *Who was to take the Ark of the Covenant to the Jordan River? (v. 8)*

   ____

   ____

   ____

3. *What happened to the Jordan when the priests stepped into the water carrying the Ark of the Covenant? (vv. 16-17)*

   ____

   ____

   ____

4. *Who stood in the middle of the Jordan as Israel passed by? (v. 17)*

___

___

___

5. *Israel crossed the Jordan on what kind of ground? (v. 17)*

___

___

___

LESSON AT-A-GLANCE

1. *The Lord is with Joshua (Joshua 3:7-8)*
2. *Joshua gives instructions before crossing (vv. 9-13)*
   A. The God of Israel is alive (vv. 9-10)
   B. The Ark of the Covenant (vv. 11-13)
3. *Israel crosses the Jordan River (vv. 14-17)*

EXPLORING THE MEANING

1. The Lord is with Joshua (Joshua 3:7-8)

In verse seven, the Lord assures Joshua that He will validate his leadership by showing the same power that He did with Moses. Israel will respect and honor Joshua and his leadership as they did with Moses. Many of those in the "new generation" of Israelites had only heard about the crossing of the Red Sea, but had not experienced this miracle of God. God said to Joshua, "Today I will begin to exalt you in the eyes of all Israel, so they may know that I am with you as I was with Moses" (v. 7, NIV). God said this in order that the new generation of people would see Him.

This brings us to the second principle of faith discovered in this passage:

Faith principle #2—"Faith" knows that God is near. That God is with the Christian is not just "head knowledge." It also includes experiences you can look back on and say, "God was with me then and His Word says He is with me NOW."

Notice how God gives instructions to Joshua concerning the priests who will carry the Ark of the Covenant (v. 8). The Ark of the Covenant, first mentioned by Moses in Exodus 25:10-22, is really a portable chest or box as the Hebrew word literally indicates. It was very elaborately constructed of acacia wood and overlaid with pure gold and was Israel's most important possession during their wilderness wanderings. It was a special holy and sacred object that signified Yahweh's Presence among His people. On top of the Ark were two cherubim (angel-like beings) with their wings facing each other, and between the cherubim was the pure gold mercy seat, representing God's Throne and Presence. Inside the Ark were three objects: 1) the tablets containing the Ten Commandments; 2) a jar of manna; and 3) Aaron's rod (Hebrews 9:4).

At first glance, it seems that God is telling the priests to carry the Ark of the Covenant and stand in the rapidly flowing Jordan River, but God has a better idea that we will detail later, when we examine verses 13-16.

2. Joshua gives instructions before crossing (vv. 9-13)

A. *The God of Israel is alive (vv. 9-10)*

In verse nine, Joshua tells Israel, "Come here and listen to the words of the Lord your God" (NIV). Joshua has a word from God for Israel. Yahweh, the God of Israel, is a God who always keeps His word. The people of Israel can be confident that when God speaks, it will come to pass. Therefore, when the Lord speaks, the people listen. This command of Joshua to Israel brings us to the third principle of faith in this passage:

Faith principle #3—"Faith" listens to the Word of God. Faith is not merely hearing words we think are from the Lord, but it is a prayerful listening and understanding of the voice of God in the midst of our situation. We must not act merely on faith in the words of men; but rather be assured that we have heard from the Word of God. To listen to another voice could mean disaster.

Joshua emphasizes the "living God" in verse 10. This, of course, is a direct reference to the surrounding nations' gods who were not alive at all, but only wooden idols. This "living God" is watchful over His people and demonstrates His love through many special acts for their benefit.

All the nations identified in verse 10 (except the Perizzites) can be found in Genesis 10, called the Tables of Nations. All these were descendants of Ham and Black people. (See "Canaanites" under *LIGHT ON THE HEAVY*).

B. *The Ark of the Covenant (vv. 11-13)*

The Children of Israel are challenged to go a step further with God and follow the Ark of the Covenant. They are told, "See, the ark of the covenant of the Lord of all the earth will go into the Jordan ahead of you" (v. 11, NIV). This action on the part of Israel leads us to the fourth principle of faith as the people attempt to cross this great obstacle:

Faith principle #4—"Faith" sees God, even in the midst of trouble. Believers see God going ahead to set up the situation, so when they arrive, God has already made a way. Believers see God even when He is not visible to others. This is the essence of vision—seeing by faith what others cannot see by sight.

The Israelites were to see the Ark of the Covenant (God's Presence) as going first into the Jordan River. At this point, the people still didn't know what to expect, but they looked to God in faith, confident in the fact that He has gone before them.

Verse 12 seems very much out of place in this context. Why does Joshua tell the people to choose 12 men, one from each tribe of Israel? There is no further explanation to the people at this time, but the people again responded in faith. The explanation of this reference is found in Joshua 4:2, 8-9. Joshua was choosing 12 men, so that after Israel crossed the Jordan they would set up a memorial to this miracle for future generations that he believed was going to occur. These men were chosen to be with Joshua before God actually did anything to the Jordan River.

Joshua also hears words of faith when his spies say, "The Lord has surely given the whole land into our hands; all the people are melting in fear because of us" (Joshua 2:24, NIV). In his excitement, Joshua begins to prepare the people early in the morning (Joshua 3:1-3). The faith of Joshua to prepare for victory before it was realized, is the fifth principle of faith.

Faith principle #5—"Faith" prepares in advance to thank God for victory. When God has spoken, believers can begin to prepare before the realization of that which was promised. Christians continue to worship and praise God as they prepare to see His work unfold before their eyes.

3. Israel crosses the Jordan River (vv. 14-17)

The promise made to Joshua and then to the people (vv.1-13) is now going to be fulfilled. How tremendous a miracle this is! The priests carrying the Ark of the Covenant now walk out into the water by faith in God's word.

The writer adds an additional note for the reader's benefit, so that the true nature of this event might be known. There are some very shallow areas of the Jordan River. Many are narrow and the water, at times, is no more than three or four feet deep. The writer adds a note about the overflow stage of the Jordan River at that time of the year. The New International Version (NIV) translates verse 15 as "Now the Jordan is at flood stage all during harvest."

The Jordan is at this "flood stage" in April and May. It is a real torrent at this time and a rushing mighty river of 12-15 feet at its narrow edges. This is the first miracle against Baal, the god of the Canaanites, who was considered the king of the Canaanite gods, because he was victorious against the sea god.

The drama continues as verses 15-16 state, "Yet as soon as. . . their [the priests] feet touched the water's edge, the water from upstream stopped flowing." Verse 13 states the promise as, "And as soon as the priests . . . set foot in the Jordan, the water flowing downstream will be cut off and stand up in a heap" (NIV). Herein lies a sixth principle of faith in this passage.

Faith principle #6—"Faith" steps in with both feet. Faith is not mere talk and idle laziness. Faith moves into action at the Word of God and trusts the Lord to honor His Word.

This miracle was good for a stretch of over 20 miles. The water was "heaped" all the way to Adam, a city 17 miles away. We do not know how God dammed up the waters 17 miles above the crossing point of Israel so that the waters leading to the Dead Sea below Israel's camp were dried up. Israel may have passed on the bed of the Jordan for a stretch of a mile or more in width. For there was no mere narrow crossing place, but a completely dry riverbed to cross on.

This great event ends in our lesson with the priests standing "firm on the dry ground in the midst of the Jordan" (v. 17). They stand as the nation passes by. The miracle of God comes to a grand completion as Israel crosses the great obstacle to their entrance into the Promised Land. If God can do this, surely He will be with them as they settle in their new homeland. This verse illustrates the seventh and last principle of faith in our lesson.

Faith principle #7—"Faith" stands firm in the middle of the struggle. When the challenges of this age seem too much for us to bear, and when faith has been tried, and when it seems as though we should give up, throw in the towel, or raise the white flag of surrender; we must still stand firm in the deliverance that God has promised. Galatians 5:1 says, "Stand fast therefore in the liberty wherewith Christ hath made us free, and be not entangled again with the yoke of bondage." Ephesians 6:13 encourages us in the power of the Lord, "having done all, to stand." If God can hold back the torrents of a mighty river, He can certainly handle any flood in the believer's life.

DISCERNING MY DUTY

1. *God said that He would "exalt" Joshua in the sight of the people (Joshua 3:7). Is it all right to ask God to "exalt" you over others?*
2. *Can the miracle of the cutting off of the Jordan be repeated today by those who exercise faith in God? Explain.*
3. *Should Christians today have a "sacred object" like the Ark of the Covenant that Israel had, so that we can be reminded of God's presence and God's power of deliverance?*
4. *What is the difference between acting in faith upon a specific Word of God to the believer, and acting on faith in what we hope God will do for us?*
5. *Faith in God and acting upon that faith has been an essential element in the life of the African American community since its earliest days. However, today some say that there is no hope; our problems are too massive for healing. How would you respond to those who say that they have no faith in the power of the African American community to be healed from the wounds of racism and its self-inflicted wounds?*

DECIDING MY RESPONSE

Select a problem in your community and resolve to act with faith to solve the problem. The action should have the specific backing of God's Word in order to be successful.

LIGHT ON THE HEAVY

CANAANITES. The Canaanites were an ancient tribe that lived in the land of Palestine before they were displaced by the nation of Israel. Along with the Amorites, the Canaanites settled the land well before 2000 B.C. Archaeological exploration of their native land and adjacent territories has provided information on many aspects of their culture. Among the numerous sites excavated in ancient Canaan, or the present-day Holy Land, are Megiddo, Jericho, and Jebus (Jerusalem).

Although both Canaanites and Amorites were established in Canaan before 2000 B.C., the Canaanites established their civilization as dominant from 2100 to 1550 B.C. Their society had several classes, ranging from the ruling nobility to the peasants. The Canaanites used a particular Cuneiform language, featuring a wedge-shaped alphabet. Their land was also dotted with walled cities. Several of these served as the centers of city-states, each having its own king, or mayor, and army.

The Canaanites are the descendants of Ham, a Black people very proud of their blackness. Reverend Walter McCray says regarding the Canaanites, "'Canaan' was the home of varied Hamitic ethnic entities. They were all known as 'Canaanites' by virtue of the land in which they lived and their ethnic roots. … These indigenous people of Canaan were Black." (*Nelson's Illustrated Bible Dictionary*, 1986, Thomas Nelson Publishers; Reverend Walter A. McCray, *The Black Presence in the Bible*, Chicago: Black Light Fellowship, 1990)

Breaking Down Walls

Based on Joshua 6

DEFINING THE ISSUE

According to the movie "Malcolm X," by the time Malcolm landed in prison, he had built around himself a solid "wall" of drugs and hatred. The concept behind the Nation of Islam was able to break down some of that wall. The Muslims were able to help break down his self-hatred by building on his hatred for the white race. But as the movie progresses, even that wall was beginning to fall. As he searched for and meditated on the truth, God revealed it to him.

Unfortunately, we come across all types of walls throughout our lives. Some are built by systems, others are built by individuals. We build walls around ourselves to enclose and protect ourselves from others. Often, that which the wall is meant to keep out is good for us and is what is needed for our spiritual betterment. Fear, jealousy, anger, selfishness, and other sins can be walls of spiritual imprisonment. Causing these kinds of walls to fall is often the first step to winning our personal battles.

AIM

By the end of the lesson, participants will be able to retell the story of Joshua and the "Battle of Jericho." They will feel a sense of victory for the Israelites and a sense of compassion for the people of Jericho. They will also begin working to tear down some of the imprisoning walls in their own lives.

SCRIPTURE TEXT

> JOSHUA 6:1 Now Jericho was straitly shut up because of the children of Israel: none went out, and none came in.
>
> 2 And the Lord said unto Joshua, See, I have given into thine hand Jericho, and the king thereof, and the mighty men of valour.
>
> 3 And ye shall compass the city, all ye men of war, and go round about the city once. Thus shalt thou do six days.
>
> 4 And seven priests shall bear before the ark seven trumpets of rams' horns: and the seventh day ye shall compass the city seven times, and the priests shall blow with the trumpets.
>
> 5 And it shall come to pass, that when they make a long blast with the ram's horn, and when ye hear the sound of the trumpet, all the people shall shout with a great shout; and the wall of the city shall fall down flat, and the people shall ascend up every man straight before him.
>
> 15 And it came to pass at the seventh day, that they rose early about the dawning of the day, and compassed the city after the same manner seven times: only on that day they compassed the city seven times.

16 And it came to pass at the seventh time, when the priests blew with the trumpets, Joshua said unto the people, Shout; for the Lord hath given you the city.

BIBLE BACKGROUND

Joshua and the Children of Israel, reminiscent of crossing over the Red Sea, had crossed over the River Jordan with the help of God. Just as crossing over the Red Sea symbolized the end of slavery and the beginning of their wanderings in the wilderness, crossing the Jordan symbolized the closing of the wilderness wanderings and the start of life in the Promised Land of Canaan. All of the men who had been born while in the wilderness and who had not been circumcised were instructed to do so. They also observed the Passover, and the manna which had fed them during their wilderness journey no longer appeared, so they ate the fruit of the land.

As Joshua approached Jericho, he was visited by an angel, the "captain of the host of the Lord" (Joshua 5:13-15). We assume his purpose was to instruct Joshua in how to capture the city successfully. As we look at the strategies Joshua used, perhaps we will be able to gain insight into how to overcome our personal "battles" in life.

POINTS TO PONDER

1. *Why was no one able to go in and out of Jericho? (Joshua 6:1)*

___

___

___

2. *What did the Lord promise Joshua? (v. 2)*

3. *What instructions did the Lord give Joshua? (vv. 3-5)*

4. *Who were the only inhabitants of the city saved and why? (v. 17)*

5. *Why were they not to keep anything accursed from the city? (v. 18)*

6. *What exceptions were there to what they could take and why? (v. 19)*

LESSON AT-A-GLANCE

1. *Jericho under siege (Joshua 6:1-2)*
2. *Strategy for battle (vv. 3-5)*
3. *Strategy followed (vv. 15-16)*

EXPLORING THE MEANING

1. Jericho under siege (Joshua 6:1-2)

The religious and moral conditions of the Canaanites were very corrupt. Daily contact with Canaanite culture further jeopardized the Israelites' moral behavior and already weak faith. Jericho was at the intersection of some important trade routes in the Jordan valley and had been a commercial center thousands of years before Joshua had come on the scene. It was a key city for the Israelites to capture. In Deuteronomy 34:3, Jericho is referred to as the "City of Palm Trees."

In Joshua 6:1, we are told that the Israelites put in place an excellent military strategy. They placed an embargo on the city. This strategy prevented supplies from reaching the people inside, thereby weakening them physically and mentally. Perhaps Joshua already visualized himself as the conqueror of Jericho. The siege was the first signal of the eventual capture of the city. Since God had stated that this event would happen, it was as if it had already occurred. This suggests that one of the first steps in dealing with our personal "walls" is to visualize ourselves past the wall and believe that with God, the battle is already won.

2. Strategy for battle (vv. 3-5)

God gives Joshua specific instructions about how the Israelites are to handle the challenge of the walls. The activity of the Israelites marching around the city once a day and seven times on the seventh day, would help to keep up the morale and physical condition of Israel's army and would unnerve the occupants of the city. To them it was probably as if God Himself was encircling the walls, and in a sense, He was. The "Ark of the covenant" was a rectangular box made of acacia wood and covered with gold. The lid or "mercy seat" was a gold plate surrounded by two cherubs with outspread wings. It was carried on poles inserted in rings at the four lower corners. Inside the Ark was a golden jar with manna, Aaron's rod, and the Ten Commandments (Hebrews 9:4). The Ark represented the presence of God (Yahweh).

The number seven is sometimes used in the Bible as the number representing completeness. When the seventh circling was done, the signal was to be given by seven priests who preceded the Ark and followed the soldiers in the procession. They were to blow seven ram's horns and all of the people were to shout, then the walls would fall.

3. Strategy followed (vv. 15-16)

Ancient cities were fortified by a thick wall that completely circled the city. Its purpose was to prevent the enemy from entering and to provide a protected firing platform for the city's defenders. Enemies would try to go over the wall with ladders, and break through the wall with tools, battering rams, or tunnel under it. By following God's instructions, the Israelites were able to evade the protection of the wall in a unique manner. Let's see if any of those instructions could apply to the "walls" we encounter.

First, all of the soldiers surrounded or encompassed the city and marched around it once a day for six days and seven times on the seventh day. To encompass means "to go around." To "go around" a situation in our lives would be to analyze all aspects of it, including our role in it. It would help us to understand fully what's involved including what's not always apparent on a superficial level. This would enable us to lay out a fully informed plan of action that will help us accomplish our goal.

Second, we are told in verse 10 that the people were instructed not to talk or make any sounds with their voice until the signal for the shout was given. Meditative silence can allow one to hear the voice of God for direction before facing the challenge of the wall.

Third, when the people went to war, the Ark reminded them of the presence of God. Prayer, fasting, and meditative Bible study are essential parts of our "compassing" of a situation. In this way, we can be guided by the Lord. He will give us insight to help us discern a correct method of approach and an effective plan of action.

Part of God's instructions included the practice of "the ban" which was devoting booty to God by destroying it. (*The Interpreter's Dictionary of the Bible*, Abingdon Press, Nashville, TN: 1984, p. 321; *The New Bible Dictionary*, Tyndale House Publishers, Inc., Wheaton, IL: 1984, p. 392). When something was accursed, it was irredeemably devoted to the Lord (Leviticus 27:28). All of the metals listed that were found in the city were to go to the Lord's treasury and the people were to be killed. However, Rahab and her family were exceptions. That's because Rahab helped two Israelite spies by hiding them and helping them to escape the king of Jericho (ch. 2). The spies promised to return the favor by saving her life when they captured the city.

Just as there were some negative things in Malcolm X's life, there were also some positive qualities hidden behind his "wall" that were worth saving. Once that wall fell, God was able to work with those qualities.

When the walls in our lives fall, we too find many qualities worth saving. These assets can best be a blessing to others, if we devote them to the Lord.

The wall that was built to protect fell from the marching and shouting of God's people. Their faith and obedience resulted in capturing the city just as God had said. Verse 21 tells us that all the people were killed along with all the animals with the exception of Rahab and her family. Fortunately for us, with Jesus' crucifixion and resurrection, destruction is no longer required. Jesus said that we should love our enemies and do good to those who treat us wrong. By God's grace, those who are our enemies can be changed into friends and allies.

In Jericho, only Rahab and her family were saved, but by the love and power of God, now whole cities could be saved (2 Corinthians 5:17).

DISCERNING MY DUTY

1. *Why did God have the Israelites topple the walls of Jericho in such an unconventional manner?*
2. *Why was it so important for the Israelites to keep themselves from the "accursed thing?" Are there any things today we would consider accursed?*
3. *Discuss the strategy the Israelites used to topple a physical wall and compare it to the type of strategy needed to topple "walls" that block our spiritual growth.*
4. *Identify some walls that our society has in place that discourage spiritual growth. What steps can the church take to help knock down these walls?*

DECIDING MY RESPONSE

Identify a "wall" in your life that is preventing you from growing spiritually or preventing you from reaching some of your God-given dreams. Meditate on these walls this week and begin to apply your situation to some of the strategies learned from today's lesson.

LIGHT ON THE HEAVY

THE BOOK OF JOSHUA. Even the casual reader of the last chapter of Deuteronomy cannot help being moved by the stirring scenes described in its 12 verses: Faithful Moses sadly views from Mount Pisgah the Promised Land which God forbids him to enter; then, aged but not weary, he dies and is buried. The children of Israel weep for him 30 days, and his epitaph is recorded for all ages, "There arose not a prophet since in Israel like unto Moses, whom the Lord knew face to face."

But the story does not end there, and as the reader instinctively glances at the next words of the holy writ, in the first verses of Joshua, he finds the drama of God's people and the land renewed in a successor to Moses, and his hopes are happily stirred. This is the reader's inspiration to study the Book of Joshua, and the pursuit of it, as he applies its many precious lessons, will prove exceedingly rewarding.

Author and Date:

The author of this sixth book of the Old Testament is nowhere identified in the Bible. Opinion of biblical scholars is divided as to whether or not Joshua, the main character of the book, also wrote it. However, the study of the book about Joshua is not hindered by the unsettled question of its authorship. Concerning some aspects of the book's authorship there can be substantial assurance and agreement:

1. The author was an eyewitness of much of the historical account. The minute details and vivid descriptions of such events as the crossing of the Jordan, the capture of Jericho, and Joshua's farewell message point to on-the-spot

observation and participation. Also, like the "we" sections of Acts, there are a few instances of autobiographical reporting, using the personal pronouns (Joshua 5:1; 5:6; 15:4).

2. The book was written very early, not long after the events themselves had transpired. This is indicated by the frequent appearance of the phrase "unto this day" and the context in which it is found. For example, Rahab, who protected the lives of Joshua's spies, was still living when the author wrote the book: "But Rahab…dwelt in the midst of Israel unto this day" (6:25).
3. Joshua is specifically identified as author of some writings. He wrote the words of a covenant which he shared with Israel "in the book of the law of God" (24:26), which was born of his farewell charge in chapter 24. Also, Joshua was responsible for the land survey of Canaan which he caused to have recorded in a book (18:9).
4. Some small parts could not have been written by Joshua. Such sections include the references to his death (24:29-30) and to the faithfulness of Israel during the years after his death (24:31). It is possible that these sections were added by Eleazar the priest, and that the note of Eleazar's death (24:33) was in turn recorded by Phinehas his son.
5. The bulk of the book was written by one author. The unity of the book as to style and organization is sufficient evidence that the book is the composition of one man, whoever he was. Jewish tradition, both ancient and modern, has consistently ascribed the authorship of the book to the man Joshua. Among Christians today, opinion is perhaps equally divided. Internally, there is nothing to deny the bulk of the book to Joshua's pen.

The important thing to recognize is that the identification of the author is not vital to the study of the book. For the book is a historical account of Israel's conquest and division of Canaan under the leadership of Joshua, with no primary autobiographical purpose of giving detailed insight into the heart of the general. If the book was of such an autobiographical purpose, identification of the author would be vital.

Place in the Old Testament:

The arrangement of the 39 books of the English Old Testament follows essentially that of the Latin Vulgate (around A.D. 400) which in turn was derived from the Greek Septuagint (third and second centuries B.C.). The books are arranged in such an order that four groups appear: Pentateuch, History, Poetry and Ethics, and Prophecy. In this arrangement, Joshua is the first of the 12 historical books. The arrangement of the Hebrew Old Testament is vastly different, though the text content is identical. The Hebrew Old Testament contains three groups, namely, Law, Prophets, and Writings. The Prophets section is divided into two parts, Former and Latter. Joshua is the first book of the Former Prophets, followed in order by Judges, Samuel (1 and 2 Samuel), and Kings (1 and 2 Kings). Placing Joshua among prophetical books may have been because its author was considered to hold the office of prophet; more likely, because the historical record illustrated the great principles which prophets preached.

Structure of Joshua:

1. Preparation for Conquest (1:1-5:15)
2. The Conquest (6:1-12:24)

3. The Inheritances (13:1-21:45)
4. The Consecration (22:1-24:33)

(Irving Jensen. *Joshua: Rest-land Won*. Chicago: Moody Press, 1966, pp. 9-12)

As for Me and My House

Based on Joshua 24

DEFINING THE ISSUE

1. You work for a popular hair care products manufacturing company and you have the opportunity to steal some products and sell them to friends for 100% profit. What do you do? Choose one of these options:
   A. Steal the products since you're underpaid and this is a way to get what's due you.
   B. Don't steal the products because you're afraid you'll get caught.
   C. Don't steal the products because you truly believe it's wrong.
2. You have developed a close relationship with a co-worker who is married. The co-worker has indicated that he really cares for you and wants you to go with him on a business trip and stay in his hotel room. You are very attracted to this person. What do you do? Choose an option:
   A. Go on the business trip. After all, it's obvious this person cares more for you than he does his spouse.
   B. Go on the business trip, but insist on your own separate hotel room.

C. Don't go on the business trip because you may be tempted to do something you believe to be wrong.

3. You and your husband have just found out that you are pregnant and you both are in your early 40s. Now that your present children are at the age of being on their own, you were looking forward to the new freedom, and a baby was not in the game plan. What do you do? Choose an option:
   A. Get an abortion, knowing that if you had the baby, you would only resent it and maybe abuse it.
   B. Have the baby and make the best of the situation.
4. The local electronics store has a device that allows you to make telephone calls from a pay phone free. What do you do? Choose an option:
   A. Buy it and use it. After all, you feel that the telephone company has ripped you off for years, so here's your opportunity to break-even.
   B. Buy it, but only use it for emergencies.
   C. Don't buy it, because you believe it is a form of stealing which is not right.

We are faced with all kinds of choices every day, like the ones listed above. Many of our choices are spiritual challenges. What we choose reveals the depths of our beliefs. An important aspect of making choices is the process we go through to get to our decision. We can learn something about this process from today's lesson.

AIM

By the end of the lesson, participants will be able to recall the story of today's episode in the life of Joshua and the steps by which he led his people to make a positive decision. They will use these steps in their own lives and in leading groups toward choices that are ethically, morally, and spiritually correct.

SCRIPTURE TEXT

> JOSHUA 24:1 And Joshua gathered all the tribes of Israel to Shechem, and called for the elders of Israel, and for their heads, and for their judges, and for their officers; and they presented themselves before God.
>
> 2 And Joshua said unto all the people, Thus saith the Lord God of Israel, Your fathers dwelt on the other side of the flood in old time, even Terah, the father of Abraham, and the father of Nachor: and they served other gods.
>
> 11 And you went over Jordan, and came unto Jericho: and the men of Jericho fought against you, the Amorites, and the Perizzites, and the Canaanites, and the Hittites, and the Girgashites, the Hivites and the Jebusites; and I delivered them into your hand.
>
> 12 And I sent the hornet before you, which drave them out from before you, even the two kings of the Amorites; but not with thy sword, nor with thy bow.
>
> 13 And I have given you a land for which ye did not labour, and cities which ye built not, and ye dwell in them; of the vineyards and olive yards which ye planted not do ye eat.
>
> 14 Now therefore fear the Lord, and serve him in sincerity and in truth: and put away the gods which your

fathers served on the other side of the flood, and in Egypt; and serve ye the Lord.

15 And if it seem evil unto you to serve the Lord, choose you this day whom ye will serve; whether the gods which your fathers served that were on the other side of the flood, or the gods of the Amorites, in whose land ye dwell: but as for me and my house, we will serve the Lord.

16 And the people answered and said, God forbid that we should forsake the Lord, to serve other gods;

24:22 And Joshua said unto the people, Ye are witnesses against yourselves that ye have chosen you the Lord, to serve him. And they said, We are witnesses.

23 Now therefore put away, said he, the strange gods which are among you, and incline your heart unto the Lord God of Israel.

24 And the people said unto Joshua, the Lord our God will we serve, and his voice will we obey.

25 So Joshua made a covenant with the people that day, and set them a statute and an ordinance in Shechem.

BIBLE BACKGROUND

The Israelites have been successful in acquiring the land of Canaan from their enemies and have not had to fight for quite awhile (Joshua 23:1). Joshua is getting older and probably knows he doesn't have much time before he dies. With this in mind, he wants to make sure that the Israelites remain faithful to God by keeping His commandments and not falling into the idolatrous worship practices of those who formerly occupied the land. Joshua wants a solid commitment from the people, not for his benefit, but for theirs. He requests that they make a choice: To whom will they be committed? As we watch how Joshua leads the Israelites into making a choice, let's think about the kinds of choices we make and what they say about what we believe.

POINTS TO PONDER

1. *Why did Joshua gather the people? (Joshua 24:1)*

 ____

 ____

 ____

2. *What are some of the things that God had done for the Israelites? (vv. 11-13)*

 ____

 ____

 ____

3. *What were the people's choices? (vv. 14-15)*

 ____

 ____

 ____

4. *What was Joshua's choice? (v. 15)*

 ____

 ____

 ____

5. *What was the people's choice? (vv. 16, 22-24)*

 ____

 ____

 ____

6. *What did Joshua do, as a result of their choice? (vv. 25-26)*

____

____

____

LESSON AT-A-GLANCE

1. *The people gathered (Joshua 24:1-2)*
2. *Their history reviewed (vv. 11-13)*
3. *The choice presented (vv. 14-15)*
4. *The people choose (vv. 16, 22-25)*
5. *The choices we make*

EXPLORING THE MEANING

1. The people gathered (Joshua 24:1-2)

Joshua has an important message from God to deliver to the Israelites. The tribes are made up of descendants of the sons of Jacob and his two grandsons through Joseph. All of them, along with their leaders, are called to meet in the city of Shechem. Everyone, regardless of their position, is challenged to make a commitment.

2. Their history reviewed (vv. 11-13)

Canaan was the fourth son/descendant of Ham whose name means "hot," "heat," and by application "black," and is regarded as the ancestor of Black people. A portion of their land was known as Canaan. Most of the peoples listed here are descendants of Canaan (Genesis 10:15-38). (Reverend Walter McCray, *The Black Presence in the Bible*, Black Light Fellowship, Chicago, IL: 1990, pp. 70 and 115).

Through Joshua, God reminds the Israelites that the successes in their battles against the people of Canaan are from Him. Reference to the "hornet" in verse 12 may either refer to the invasion of the Israelites being preceded by a plague of insects with painful and maybe fatal stings, or it may symbolically refer to the rumors of their victories which spread before their arrival. (Reverend J. R. Dummelow, ed., *The One Volume Bible Commentary*, MacMillan Publishing Co., Inc., New York, NY: 1978, p. 154)

But, their victories could not be attributed to the Israelites' skill as warriors, nor their great weapons. The land they occupied had not been earned by them, the cities they lived in had not been built by them, and they were eating food that they had not grown.

Joshua prepared the people for the challenge of the choice. He reminded them of all that God had done for them and that He was the source of all they had.

When faced with challenging choices, our own process of choosing should first include recalling all that God has done for us and seeing all that God has provided for us.

3. The choice presented (vv. 14-15)

Joshua's decision was for God. In stating the choice, Joshua first presents his choice, regarding his own partiality and what he hopes they will choose. Then he presents the alternative. He indicates what that choice entails, so that there is no misunderstanding.

The Israelites had been exposed to three forms of idolatry: One form (the teraphin statues, one of which Rachel stole from Laban; Genesis 31:19, 30) was the ancestral worship of Mesopotamian forefathers. Another was animal worship. Some of the Israelites had practiced animal worship while in Egypt. They displayed the golden calf or apis bull, as a result (Exodus 32). Finally, the Baalism of the Canaanite tribes was a constant temptation to Israel. (Reverend J. R. Dummelow, ed., *The One Volume Bible Commentary*, MacMillan Publishing Co., Inc., New York, NY: 1978)

If the Israelites chose God, idol worship would have to be forsaken. The choice would mean the decision would be for God alone, completely respectful, sincere, and truthful in their acknowledgment and service to Him.

Joshua then posed a paradox to the people that revealed his choice and expressed how ridiculous any other choice but God would be. "If they believed God to be evil," he said, "then their choice should be made accordingly." But Joshua made quite clear his own choice, for himself and his household.

The second step in making our own decision is to evaluate what our choice will say about our view of God. If we believe God to be evil and we say we are His, then our choice will reflect that. However, if we have a loving respect for Him and are committed to serving Him with sincerity and truthfulness, our choice will reflect that decision: love and faithfulness to Him.

4. The people choose (vv. 16, 22-25)

In declaring their choice, the people call on God for His support. To emphasize the seriousness of their decision, Joshua reiterates clearly what they have chosen. In a legal sense, they are their own witnesses. The purpose of a witness is to attest to the truth about themselves and about God. The people agreed to condemn themselves if they break this agreement. Instructions are given to them to assure that they keep this covenant. First, they must get rid of all their idols. Second, they must give God their wholehearted obedience and service. Joshua documents the agreement in the form of a law.

5. The choices we make

When making decisions where moral or spiritual choices are involved, ask yourself these questions:

1. Has God been good to me?
2. What choice would Jesus, my spiritual role model, make?
3. What message will my choice send about my love for God and the church?
4. How will my choice affect my Christian worship and ministry?

The key to effective decision making is total honesty with ourselves. We must not rationalize choices that are against God's will with phrases like, "God knows my heart" because He truly does. Once we make the decision to obey and serve God with our total being, all that we say and do, and all that we do not say and do not do, should be based on our commitment. We are witnesses for or against ourselves. We can call on God for strength and discernment in making choices, but the final decision is ours. If we commit ourselves to God, we can be sure He is already committed to us.

DISCERNING MY DUTY

1. *What was Joshua forcing the people to do when he demanded a choice from them? What did it mean when he asked them to incline their hearts to God?*
2. *What does presenting oneself before the Lord include? What purpose does it serve?*
3. *What is the significance of being a witness against yourself?*

4. *Why does Joshua refer to the gods as "strange" in verse 23, contrasted to "the Lord our God" in verse 24?*
5. *What are some of the "strange gods" that we worship or are tempted to worship in our time?*
6. *On our jobs, in our neighborhoods, in various organizations, and in our church groups, people are challenged to make choices. What can you learn from Joshua regarding the steps to take in leading a group to take a positive stand on an issue?*

DECIDING MY RESPONSE

Sit down this week and consider a personal issue you have been vacillating on that is challenging you spiritually. Apply what you've learned from this week's lesson that will help you to come to the right decision. If there is nothing challenging you presently, write down specific steps you can follow, steps you learned from this lesson. This will help you make the right decision when such a situation arises in your life.

LIGHT ON THE HEAVY

JOSHUA'S CLOSING MINISTRY.
Covenant Renewal (24:1-28)

Joshua 24:1-28 records the final ministry of Joshua to his beloved people. His dying wish was that they would burn four great impressions on their heart and in their life: covenant, history, present blessing, and consecration.

1. Covenant:

   This was the reason for gathering Israel to Shechem. Shechem was the place that suggested the original covenant made by God with His people. God first promised Canaan to Abram (Genesis 12:6-7); Jacob built an altar (33:20); and Joshua built an altar and renewed Israel's covenant relationship with God (Joshua 8:30- 35). Joshua's appeal to Israel was that they rest on the foundation of the covenant. At the end of his speech on this momentous day, "Joshua made a covenant with the people...and set them a statute and an ordinance in Shechem" (24:25).

2. History:

   Joshua's appeal was that they remember history. From the divine call of Israel's father Abraham to their inheritance of the land, God was the Gracious Deliverer (24:2-12).

3. Present Blessings:

   "Count your present blessings" is the effect of the few words of 24:13. Israel was now enjoying the gift of a fruitful land to dwell in.

4. Consecration:

   This was the appeal to the will, and Joshua did not intend to let the people make their choice lightly. The dialogue proceeded in this order:

   a. The clear option: "Choose you this day whom ye will serve"— Jehovah, or the gods (24:14-15).
   b. Joshua's example: "As for me and my house, we will serve Jehovah" (24:15).
   c. Israel's hasty commitment: "We also will serve Jehovah" (24:18). There was no flaw in the words of this commitment. But Joshua sensed that the words were probably spoken too quickly, without due deliberation,

and the words "far be it from us that we should forsake the Lord" (v. 16, NIV) had the sound of dangerous self-confidence.

d. Joshua's challenge: "Ye cannot serve the Lord: for He is an Holy God" (24:19). The sole purpose of this strong statement was to disarm Israel's self-righteousness.
e. Israel's deliberate insistence: "Nay; but we will serve the Lord" (24:21).

When Joshua was satisfied with the genuineness of the people's consecration, he solemnly renewed the covenant, laid down statues and decrees for them, wrote the precepts in the Book of God's law, and "he took a large stone and set it up there beneath the oak [tree] near the holy place of the Lord" (24:26, NIV), which would be a witness to the people's renewal of their consecration to God.

Joshua's earthly ministry thus came to a close. Satisfied that his people's consecration was in earnest, he "let the people depart, every man unto his inheritance" (24:28).

APPENDIX (24:29-33)

The words appended to the Book of Joshua recording the burial of three of God's servants Joshua, Joseph, and Eleazar are a fitting conclusion to the theme of the book. (Irving Jensen, *Joshua: Rest-Land Won*, Chicago: Moody Press, 1966, pp. 112, map, 122-124, text)

About The Author

Dr. Melvin E. Banks is the founder of Urban Ministries, Inc., the largest African-American Christian media and content provider, serving over 50,000 churches with curriculum, books, magazines, Bible studies, videos, teaching resources, and more.

Alabama native Dr. Banks began his spiritual journey at the age of 12, sharing Bible stories with younger children and traveling with his mentor to Birmingham's remote parts to give his testimony to adults. Inspired by Hosea 4:6, where God says, "My people are destroyed from lack of knowledge," he established UMI in 1970 to publish positive images of African-Americans in the biblical experience. During its first 12 years, UMI operated from the basement of the Banks' home, and Dr. Banks marketed his first Sunday School curriculum, *InTeen*, to churches out of his car's trunk.

Dr. Banks received an honorary doctorate from his alma mater, Wheaton College, where he served as a trustee for many years. Moody Bible Institute honored him as an Alumnus of the year, and Dr. Banks was recognized for his achievements by the History Makers Foundation.

Today UMI's innovative work has led to many publishers becoming more ethnically and racially diverse in their efforts. Materials include Sunday School curriculum, Vacation Bible School resources, books, videos, music, and website UrbanFaith.com – all of which speak to people of color in the context of their culture. For more information, please visit UrbanMinistries.com.

Made in the USA
Middletown, DE
10 May 2022

65608713R00099